DATE DUE			

GRAHAM GREENE

Literature and Life Series
[Formerly Modern Literature and World Dramatists]

Selected list of titles:

JAMES BALDWIN	*Carolyn Wedin Sylvander*
ANTHONY BURGESS	*Samuel Coale*
TRUMAN CAPOTE	*Helen S. Garson*
WILLA CATHER	*Dorothy Tuck McFarland*
T. S. ELIOT	*Burton Raffel*
E. M. FORSTER	*Claude J. Summers*
ERNEST HEMINGWAY	*Samuel Shaw*
JOHN IRVING	*Gabriel Miller*
CHRISTOPHER ISHERWOOD	*Claude J. Summers*
HENRY JAMES, THE NOVELS OF	*Edward Wagenknecht*
HENRY JAMES, THE TALES OF	*Edward Wagenknecht*
KEN KESEY	*Barry H. Leeds*
ARTHUR KOESTLER	*Mark Levene*
D. H. LAWRENCE	*George J. Becker*
DORIS LESSING	*Mona Knapp*
MARY McCARTHY	*Willene Schaefer Hardy*
NORMAN MAILER	*Philip H. Bufithis*
JOHN O'HARA	*Robert Emmet Long*
EUGENE O'NEILL, THE PLAYS OF	*Virginia Floyd*
GEORGE ORWELL	*Roberta Kalechofsky*
EDGAR ALLAN POE	*Bettina L. Knapp*
MURIEL SPARK	*Velma Bourgeois Richmond*
JOHN STEINBECK	*Paul McCarthy*
LIONEL TRILLING	*Edward Joseph Shoben, Jr.*
MARK TWAIN	*Robert Keith Miller*
GORE VIDAL	*Robert F. Kiernan*
ROBERT PENN WARREN	*Katherine Snipes*
EDMUND WILSON	*David Castronovo*
THOMAS WOLFE	*Elizabeth Evans*
VIRGINIA WOOLF	*Manly Johnson*

Complete list of titles in the series available from publisher on request.

GRAHAM GREENE

Richard Kelly

FREDERICK UNGAR PUBLISHING CO.
NEW YORK

Copyright © 1984 by Frederick Ungar Publishing Co., Inc.
Printed in the United States of America

Library of Congress Cataloging in Publication Data
Kelly, Richard Michael, 1937–
    Graham Greene.

    Bibliography: p.
    Includes index.
    1. Greene, Graham, 1904–   —Criticism and
interpretation.   I. Title.
PR6013.R44Z6345   1984   823'.912   84-8595
ISBN 0-8044-2464-0

Excerpts from *The Living Room* by Graham Greene,
copyright © 1953 by Viking Penguin, Inc.; *The Potting
Shed* by Graham Greene, copyright © 1959 by Viking
Penguin, Inc.; and *The Complaisant Lover* by Graham
Greene, copyright © 1959 by Viking Penguin, Inc. are
reprinted by permission of Viking Penguin, Inc.

Contents

GRAHAM GREENE

1

The Man and His Work

Graham Greene's earliest memory of his childhood contains the seed of pity that was to grow into an obsessive theme in his major novels: "The first thing I remember is sitting in a pram at the top of a hill with a dead dog lying at my feet." His sister's pug had been run over by a carriage, and his nurse thought it convenient to wheel the body back home. Greene's mother once told him that among his first spoken words months later was the phrase "poor dog."

He was born on October 2, 1904, at Berkhamsted, Hertfordshire, and was the fourth of six children. His father, Charles Henry Greene, was a history and classics master who, in 1910, became headmaster at Berkhamsted School. "As a headmaster," Greene later wrote, "he was even more distant than our aloof mother." His memory of his mother was of a "cool puritan beauty—she seemed to eliminate all confusion, to recognize the good from the bad and choose the good." For the first eight years of his life, Greene enjoyed his childhood in the small village atmosphere of Berkhamsted, visiting his large number of cousins, aunts, and uncles who lived nearby. At his uncle's house in Harston he suddenly discovered that he could read, and the book that stirred the revelation was *Dixon Brett,*

Detective. In order to protect his discovery, he read only in secret, in a remote attic. Before long he was enjoying such books as *The Little Duke* by Charlotte Yonge (which later plays a part in his novel *The Ministry of Fear*), *The Children of the Forest* by Captain Frederick Marryat, the Andrew Lang Fairy Books, Rudyard Kipling's *Baa Baa, Black Sheep*, and the stories of Beatrix Potter.

As Greene himself notes, "the influence of early books is profound. So much of the future lies on the shelves: early reading has more influence on the conduct than any religious teaching." Some of the books he read as a young boy that were to chart his future included Rider Haggard's *King Solomon's Mines* and *Montezuma's Daughter*, the story of Cortez's retreat; Stanley Weyman's *The Story of Francis Claude*, about the persecution of Protestants during Queen Mary's reign; and Captain Gibson's *The Lost Column*, about the Boxer rebellion. Greene believes that his later urge to visit Liberia and Mexico and to write such novels as *The Heart of the Matter* and *The Power and the Glory* derived from his boyhood reading of these exciting and exotic adventure stories.

In 1912, as he approached his eighth birthday, Greene was enrolled in Berkhamsted School. He was to spend the next ten years there, the last five of which proved to be a hellish confinement for him. Being the headmaster's son, he felt himself alienated from the other boys: "I had left civilization behind and entered a savage country of strange customs and inexplicable cruelties: a country in which I was a foreigner and a suspect, quite literally a hunted creature." He soon became a regular truant who would hide in the hollow of a hawthorn hedge so that he could read, safely removed from the monotony, humiliation, and pain generated by the school. His rebellion was aroused by "loneliness, the struggle of conflicting loyalties, the sense of continuous grime, of unlocked lavatory doors, the odor of farts." He felt imprisoned, as if his childhood had been fatally betrayed.

The public schools at this time were notorious for warping the sexuality of their students. The schoolmasters, trained under the strict, puritanical codes of the Victorian period, conveyed consciously or unconsciously through their lessons and regulations the idea that sex was dirty and unpleasant and that the human body was repulsive. The lavatory doors at Berkhamsted had no locks so that the boys could not engage in any sexual activities. Greene points out, however, that "it was a very pure house, there was no hint of homosexuality." This sexually repressive atmosphere had a powerful and lasting impact on Greene and helped to shape the peculiar sexuality of his literary figures. Very few of his characters enjoy sex; rather, their eroticism evokes fear, guilt, and revulsion, and is usually depicted (very discreetly) in squalid or secret surroundings. Greene's negative attitude toward homosexuality similarly derives from this early period. The few homosexuals who appear in his fiction are portrayed as threatening, selfish, cruel, and untrustworthy. Like Berkhamsted itself, Greene's fiction embodies a puritanical tone that keeps it "a very pure house."

During these younger days he developed a terror of birds and bats, and a fear of death by drowning. A nearby canal conveyed to him a sense of danger: "the menace of insulting words from strange brutal canal workers with blackened faces like miners . . . and the danger, too, as I believe, of death from drowning." Many of his early dreams were of a watery death, and years later two of his early novels, *England Made Me* and *Brighton Rock*, reflected his fear in the fate of their heroes, Anthony Farrant and Pinkie Brown, both of whom drown. Greene's growing insecurity and anxiety were especially embodied in a recurrent nightmare about a witch who would lurk at night on the nursery landing by the linen cupboard. His dreams became an important part of his imaginative life and served him well in later years when he had acquired the skill of a writer, which he could use like a talisman to manipulate and exorcise these early demons of childhood.

The young Greene began seeking desperate avenues of escape from his growing depression. He drank a glass of hypo under the false impression that it was poisonous enough to kill him. He made later attempts to take his own life by drinking hay-fever medicine, eating some deadly nightshade, and swallowing some twenty aspirins. His behavior continued to grow more eccentric and self-destructive until his father, in 1920, finally decided that the boy required psychoanalysis. He put his son under the care of an analyst named Kenneth Richmond, and for the next six months the boy acquired his sought-after freedom from the public school and enjoyed one of the happiest periods of his life.

When he returned to school he found it easier to make friends. He escaped the "petty gangsters" of the sixth form and enjoyed the company of more sophisticated young men, such as Peter Quennell, who went on to become a distinguished man of letters. At this time Greene began writing sentimental fantasies and one-act plays. One of his stories, called "The Tick of the Clock," was published in the school magazine. Greene's spirits were high: "Now, I told myself, I was really a professional writer. . . . The sense of glory touched me for the first and last time."

In 1922 he entered Balliol College, Oxford, to study history. In his own words he was at this time "a muddled adolescent who wanted to write but hadn't found his subject, who wanted to express his lust, but was too scared to try, and who wanted to love but hadn't found a real object." When he rejoined his family during the summer of 1923, however, he fell in love with the governess assigned to care for his younger brother and sister. She was about thirty years old, some ten years older than he: "she was lying on the beach and her skirt had worked up high and showed a long length of naked thigh. Suddenly at that moment I fell in love, body and mind." Her plans to marry another man, however, soon frustrated Greene's adolescent passion, and his manic-depressive tendency from earlier years returned with renewed force.

Greene described himself at this time as an inhabitant of two symbolic countries—innocence and experience, heaven and hell: "you had to step carefully: the border was close beside your gravel path." During this period, however, Greene's depression ruled his world. As he says, "One began to believe in heaven because one believed in hell, but for a long while it was only hell one could picture with a certain intimacy." As a writer Greene was later able to deal with his manic-depressive states by incorporating them into his mythic vision of the world. He embodied his psychic dualism in his fictional characters who cross and recross the elusive border between joy and pain, peace and torment, goodness and evil. His opposing moods were also manifested in the very nature of the novels themselves. Greene observes that "If *A Burnt-Out Case* in 1961 represented the depressive side of a manic-depressive writer, *Travels with My Aunt* eight years later surely represented the manic at its height—or depth."

It was in the autumn of 1923 that Greene, in a confused state of intolerable boredom and sexual frustration, took his older brother's revolver, slipped a bullet into and spun its chamber, aimed its muzzle into his right ear, and pulled the trigger. The excitement of gambling with his own life rejuvenated him: "I remember an extraordinary sense of jubilation, as if carnival lights had been switched on in a drab street. . . . It was like a young man's first successful experience of sex." During the next few months he played this dangerous game five more times. His addiction to these adrenaline ecstasies soon abated, but his acute fear of boredom and his penchant for danger to diminish that fear remained with him. His later excursions into Africa, Mexico, and Vietnam during bloody revolutions, for example, were largely sponsored by the same dreadful feeling of emptiness in his life that he sought to overcome by this new form of Russian roulette.

Greene's academic career was not especially distinguished. He received a moderate second in his modern history finals and was editor of the *Oxford Outlook*. During his last year at Oxford, in 1925, he published a volume of verse entitled *Babbling April*, a work that is derivative of the style of Edna St. Vincent Millay. After he graduated from Oxford he had no clear future mapped out. He worked for a couple of weeks for the British-American Tobacco Company, became fascinated with the novels of Joseph Conrad, and began writing a novel under Conrad's influence about the Carlist refugees in London and a young Englishman involved in their conspiracy.

He finally decided on a career in journalism, but no London newspaper was willing to take on an apprentice at the time. So, in 1926 he moved to Nottingham where he worked without salary for the

Nottingham Journal. In one of his film reviews for the paper he made a misstatement of fact about Catholic dogma, and a young woman reader named Vivien Dayrell-Browning wrote him a letter correcting his theology. The correspondence led to a meeting, friendship, and finally marriage. Before Greene married, however, he took instructions in the Catholic faith in order to understand and appreciate better the beliefs of his future wife. In February 1926, he was formally received into the Roman Catholic church. He took his baptismal name after Thomas, the doubter.

By March of 1926 Greene had been hired as subeditor for *The Times,* where he happily stayed for the next four years. Although his journalistic duties were routine, they helped to sharpen his style as a novelist. His evening chores—removing the clichés of reporters, compressing stories to minimal length, and gaining insights into an array of new personalities—all contributed to his morning work on a novel called *The Man Within.* It is the story of a hunted man involved in a web of smuggling, treachery, murder, and suicide. Accepted by the distinguished publishing firm of William Heinemann, it was published in 1929 and sold more than eight thousand copies, a remarkable success for a first novel. Later Greene was to write that the work "is very young and very sentimental. It has no meaning for me today and I can see no reason for its success." His attitude at the time, however, was quite different. When he visited the publishing firm to discuss his first contract, Greene remembers sitting "on the edge of the chair ready to leap up. The bearded ghost of [Joseph] Conrad rumbled on the rooftops with the rain."

Stirred by his initial success, Greene determined to leave *The Times* to become a professional

author. He was helped in the decision by his publisher, who offered him six hundred pounds a year
for three years in return for three novels. And so he
confidently entered a brave new world: "I left *The
Times* the author of a successful first novel. I
thought I was a writer already and that the world
was at my feet, but life wasn't like that."

If he saw the writing of his first novel as an
adventure, the writing of the second, *The Name of
Action*, he viewed as a duty. Both this novel, published in 1930, and the next one, *Rumour at Nightfall* (1931), were awkward action stories whose characters failed to come alive. Greene has now
withdrawn these two works from his bibliography
and obviously regrets having published them.

Having, as he said, "squandered" his three
years of security, Greene began writing book reviews for *The Spectator*, a job he continued until
the early 1940s. But having written two unsuccess-
ful novels and a biography of Lord Rochester, which
Heinemann turned down, Greene finally achieved
notice with the next novel, *Stamboul Train* (entitled
Orient Express in the United States), the third book
in the three-year contract, which had now expired.
Greene acknowledged that in 1931 "for the first and
last time in my life I deliberately set out to write a
book to please, one which with luck might be made
into a film." He succeeded in achieving both aims.
Stamboul Train was published in 1932 and was selected by the English Book Society, guaranteeing a
sale of at least ten thousand copies, and then 20th
Century–Fox acquired the novel to use as the basis
for a film.

Greene had begun writing his next novel, *It's
a Battlefield*, before the publication of *Stamboul
Train*. The germ for this story came from a dream:
"I was condemned to prison for five years and I

woke depressed by the thought that my wife would be over thirty when we lived with each other again." The novel did not sell many copies, and it remains the least read of all his books. Published in 1934, this work extends the theme of betrayal and responsibility that appeared in *The Man Within* to attack the social injustice and hypocrisy of contemporary institutions. Greene's next novel, *England Made Me* (entitled *The Shipwrecked* in the United States), also suggests his dismal view of a godless society, and introduced the rather daring subject of incest.

During the winter of 1934–35 Greene and his twenty-three-year-old cousin Barbara set out on a rugged trip to Liberia. The ostensible purpose of the journey was to write a travel book, but the work that emerged, *Journey without Maps* (1936), is really much more than that. Greene's excursion was an attempt to escape his routine work in London and to put himself on a dangerous edge of life in order to understand more fully the unexplored regions of his mind and to revitalize his creative instincts. *Journey without Maps*, then, might best be read as a psychological quest. As Greene writes, "there are times of impatience, when one is less content to rest at the urban stage, when one is willing to suffer some discomfort for the chance of finding—there are a thousand names for it, King Solomon's Mines, the 'heart of darkness' . . . or one's place in time, based on a knowledge not only of one's present but of the past from which one has emerged." Significantly, Greene had long conceptualized Africa as a shape, roughly that of the human heart.

Another aspect of Greene's motivation to walk into the heart of Liberia has special relevance to many of his novels, and that is his attempt to return to the simplicity of childhood. A recurrent theme in

Greene's writing is that of betrayed innocence. It can be seen in such books as *The Man Within*, *The Ministry of Fear*, *The Heart of the Matter*, *A Burnt-Out Case*, and *The Honorary Consul*, to name a few. Somewhere in Greene's own youth he appears to have experienced a profound hurt to his sensibility, and he has subsequently become obsessed with the difference between the way the world should be and the way it actually is. In this light, *Journey without Maps* can be read as an attempt to recover the sense of innocence that has been blighted by civilization. As Greene says, "Freud has made us conscious as we have never been before of those ancestral threads which still exist in our unconscious minds to lead us back." Greene suggests that he shared the same psychological compulsion to explore Africa as did Livingstone, Stanley, Rimbaud, and Conrad: "The writers . . . were conscious of this purpose, but one is not certain how far the explorers knew the nature of the fascination which worked on them in the dirt, the disease, the barbarity and the familiarity of Africa." To walk into the center of Africa is to walk into the past, the starting point where Greene discovered "the finer taste, the finer pleasure, the finer terror on which we might have built."

After he returned to the "seedy level" of the African coast, characterized by dishonesty, treachery, and crime introduced by European trade, he reflected, "This journey, if it had done nothing else, had reinforced a sense of disappointment with what man had made out of childhood." Years later, Greene's fictional heroes continue to pursue the lost world, Querry (in a *Burnt-Out Case*) in a leper colony and Scobie (in *The Heart of the Matter*) in the sweltering tropics of South Africa. More subtly, however, many of Greene's characters seek the past through their attraction to the seedy aspects of life. As Greene explains it, "This may be the deep appeal of the seedy. It *is* nearer the beginning; like Monrovia [a city on the Liberian coast] its building has begun wrong, but at least it has only begun; it hasn't reached so far away as the smart, the new, the chic, the cerebral."

In 1935 *The Spectator* assigned Greene to be its regular film critic. During the next four and a half years he watched more than four hundred movies. The cinema proved to be another escape from the routine difficulty of writing novels, but at the same time the novels he worked on during these years show the influences of cinematographic techniques. In 1938 one of his reviews for *Night and Day*, a magazine he co-edited for six months, led to a much publicized lawsuit. He had suggested that in *Wee Willie Winkie* Shirley Temple "had a certain adroit coquetry which appealed to middle-aged men." Her studio, 20th Century–Fox, claimed that he had accused them of "procuring" Miss Temple "for immoral purposes" and won its case. The motion picture company received over a thousand pounds and Miss Temple two thousand.

Having enjoyed the financial success and public adulation earned from *Stamboul Train*, Greene tried his hand at another thriller, *A Gun for Sale* (entitled *This Gun for Hire* in the United States), published in 1936. Believing that the moral climate of his boyhood, with its emphasis on patriotism, had vanished in the mid-thirties, Greene set out to write a melodramatic story about a hunted man "out to revenge himself for all the dirty tricks of life, not to save his country."

Greene expanded his writing schedule to include some prentice film scripts for Alexander Korda, *The Green Cockatoo* and *The First and The*

Last, based on John Galsworthy's short story. About
this time he was also beginning another novel called
Brighton Rock when his publisher commissioned
him to report on the religious persecution of Catholics in Mexico. He spent the winter of 1938 in Tabasco and Chiapas and recorded his journey
through these religiously oppressed provinces in
The Lawless Roads (called *Another Mexico* in the
United States). Many of the characters and settings
in this account reappear in Greene's later masterpiece, *The Power and the Glory*.

With the publication of *Brighton Rock* in 1938
the critics discovered that Greene was a Catholic
writer. Of course, all of his novels were written after
he became a Catholic in 1926, but during his stay
in Mexico where he completed *Brighton Rock*, he
had, in his words, "discovered some emotional belief, among the empty and ruined churches from
which the priests had been excluded." The twisted
Catholicism of the novel's hero, Pinkie, and the
saintly innocence of his girlfriend, Rose, clearly derive from Greene's emotional involvement with the
outlawed church.

After his return from Mexico, Greene, in a spurt
of creativity, wrote *The Confidential Agent* in six
weeks. One of the few books of his own that he cares
to reread, *The Confidential Agent* was an attempt
"to create something legendary out of a contemporary thriller: the hunted man who becomes in
turn the hunter." He wrote the book quickly because of his anxiety that Germany would soon in-
vade England. He feared that he would be called
into the military and that his family would be left
without support. Determined to write another "entertainment," as he called his thrillers, as quickly
as possible to bolster his family's finances, he took
Benzedrine for breakfast for six weeks and suffered

the results of physical and psychological depression. In the afternoons he worked at a more leisurely pace on *The Power and the Glory*, the book that gave Greene more satisfaction than any other he had previously written.

Published in England in 1940, the first edition of *The Power and the Glory* was limited to a mere thirty-five-hundred copies. Published in the United States under the title *The Labyrinthine Ways*, it sold only about two thousand copies. The growing war in Europe, of course, was one of the reasons for the small printings and sales. After the war the novel became a huge success in France, due in large part to the famous novelist François Mauriac's strong praise for the work. Then the American director John Ford turned the novel into a film called *The Fugitive*, starring Henry Fonda. In the 1950s the book won critical acclaim in America, and today many people consider it Greene's finest achievement. The story of a hunted "whisky priest" with an illegitimate daughter, the novel brought a strong reaction from the Holy Office, the church's tribunal for the protection of faith and morals, which condemned the book because it was "paradoxical" and "dealt with extraordinary circumstances." Years later, however, when the author met Pope Paul VI, the pontiff remarked, according to Greene, that he had read the book and went on to say, "Mr. Greene, some parts of your books are certain to offend some Catholics, but you should pay no attention to that." In 1941 the novel was awarded the distinguished Hawthornden Prize.

By 1941 Greene had become the literary editor and drama critic for *The Spectator* and worked in the Ministry of Information in London. Then, in the winter of 1941, he was recruited into the Secret Service and sent to West Africa, where he wrote his

next "entertainment," *The Ministry of Fear*. An espionage story filled with melodramatic and bizarre
twists, it compensated for the dull routine of
Greene's actual assignment as a secret service
agent: "my days were spent coding and decoding
in an office and my nights were passed with a col-
league in a disused police bungalow on a mosquito-
haunted creek. To cheer ourselves we used to hunt
cockroaches by the light of electric torches."

After nearly a year in Sierra Leone, West Africa,
Greene returned to London to continue another
year in the intelligence sector of the Foreign Office.
Then, in 1944, he was appointed to the board of
directors of the publishing house of Eyre and Spot-
tiswoode. He remained a director until 1948, eval-
uating manuscripts for the publisher. After the war,
in 1946, Greene began work on his next book, *The
Heart of the Matter*, one of his major novels. In 1947
he published a collection of nineteen short stories
and in the following year *The Heart of the Matter*
appeared, his first serious novel in eight years. During the winter of 1948 he was a guest speaker with
François Mauriac at Les Grandes Conférences
Catholiques in Brussels. Among Europeans and
Americans, Greene's reputation as a Catholic novelist spread quickly, and his latest novel led Catholic critics to argue among themselves as to whether
its hero, Scobie, was saved or damned by God.
Greene began to receive numerous letters, especially from women and priests, requesting his counsel about their marital or religious problems.
Greene was hounded by the religious public for
years after the novel appeared, and he wrote later:
"I felt myself used and exhausted by the victims of
religion." Greene found the label "Catholic writer"
detestable, and to this day declares himself "not a

Catholic writer but a writer who happens to be a Catholic."

When the motion picture producer Alexander Korda wanted to make a film about the four-power occupation of Vienna, he sent Greene to that city for three weeks to research the subject. During the last two days of his trip Greene heard about a diluted penicillin racket and was given a tour of the massive sewer system of the city. The two ideas came together, and he had the story for *The Third Man*, one that was quite different from Korda's original concept. Nevertheless, Greene was given a free hand to develop his mysterious tale of the corrupt Harry Lime, and the motion picture, released in 1950, turned out to be one of the most successful. in Greene's career.

In 1951 Greene went to Malaya on assignment for *Life* magazine, and in the same year he published *The End of the Affair*. All in all, the fifties were a period of great unrest for Greene. He acknowledged that "it became a habit with me to visit troubled places, not to seek material for novels, but to regain the sense of insecurity which I had enjoyed in the three blitzes on London." After his trip to Malaya for *Life*, he spent four winters in Vietnam between 1951 and 1955, reporting the French Wars for the *Sunday Times* (London) and *Figaro*. In 1953 he went to Kenya to report on the Mau Mau uprising for the *Sunday Times*. Three years later he visited Stalinist Poland and then Haiti in 1956. In 1958 he traveled to the Belgian Congo to study life in a leper colony and later went on to Cuba to investigate the social and political unrest of that country. No matter what Greene's motivations were for such extensive travel to dangerous countries, at least four books resulted from the journeys: *The Quiet American* in

1955, *Our Man in Havana* in 1958, *A Burnt-Out Case* in 1961, and *The Comedians* in 1966.

The roles of the journalist and novelist were beginning to merge. Greene wrote that "Perhaps there is more direct reportage in *The Quiet American* than in any other novel I have written." The political theme of that book sometimes overwhelmed its merit as fiction. A. J. Liebling in *The New Yorker*, for example, condemned Greene for accusing the United States of murder in Vietnam by supplying explosives to General Thé, a leader of a band of anticommunist rebels.[1] Greene's anti-Americanism is dramatized in several of his novels besides *The Quiet American*. In *The Comedians*, for example, the American characters represent a shallow culture and foolish political policy. In 1967, in a letter to *The Times*, he wrote "If I had to choose between life in the Soviet Union and life in the United States of America, I would certainly choose the Soviet Union." And later, in 1970, Greene publicized his protest against American involvement in Southeast Asia by resigning from the American Academy of Arts.

Greene's anti-Americanism is, in part, an expression of his cultural snobbery, which has intensified over the years. The English critic John Atkins satirically captures this aspect of Greene's character: "At first only Catholics will pass muster, then American Catholics are excluded, and in time we are left with French Catholics alone. Later he will confine himself to French Catholics who have been purified by the pangs of adultery, and it will probably end with a select circle of adulterous French Catholics who know the Devil personally."

Before he published another major work, Greene wrote two plays, *The Living Room* (1953) and *The Potting Shed* (1957). Like his novels, they deal with characters who have to face serious religious questions. Although a latecomer to the theater, Greene said that his life as a writer "is littered with discarded plays, as it is littered with discarded novels." Greene went on to write and have produced several comic and farcical plays, including *The Complaisant Lover, Carving a Statue,* and *The Return of A. J. Raffles.*

Greene got the idea for his next novel, *Our Man in Havana,* in his little shack in Freetown, Sierra Leone, where he worked for the Foreign Office coding and decoding messages from London. He wrote the first draft of the story in the 1940s but used Estonia instead of Cuba for the setting. In the earlier version it was the extravagance of the hero's wife, not his daughter, that led him to cheat the secret service. But Greene recast the story after he visited Havana in the 1950s: "it struck me that here in this extraordinary city, where every vice was permissible and every trade possible, lay the true background for my comedy." Although the novel is a satire of the British Intelligence Service, the Cubans were angered by the book because they felt it failed to take seriously the justice of their revolution against the Batista government.

When Greene was en route to the Belgian Congo in 1959 he had the beginning of a story line for a new novel in his mind: "a stranger turns up in a remote leper settlement for no apparent reason." Once at the leprosarium, Greene took copious notes in order to establish an authentic medical background for *A Burnt-Out Case* and became in the process close friends with Dr. Michel Lechat, the physician of the settlement. Greene recalled that "Never had a novel proved more recalcitrant or more depressing." After the publication of *A Burnt-Out Case,* Evelyn Waugh, the well-known contem-

porary Catholic novelist, wrote Greene saying that
he identified the hero of the novel, a famous Catholic architect who abandoned his profession and his
faith to live among the lepers in the Congo, with
Greene himself. Greene vigorously denied the relationship and denied, too, that he had Waugh in
mind when he drew the character of Ryker, a gro-
tesquely pious Catholic. Members of the Catholic
press were upset with the novel because they assumed that Greene, like his hero, Querry, had lost
his faith. Greene was infuriated by this sort of criticism, insisted that a novelist is not a moral teacher
or a theologian, and asserted, "If people are so im-
petuous as to regard this book as a recantation of
faith I cannot help it. Perhaps they will be surprised
to see me at Mass."

In 1958 Greene was appointed to the board of
directors of the Bodley Head publishing firm and
for the next ten years read numerous manuscripts
and helped to decide which new authors were to be
published. Besides the enormous popularity his
novels won for him among Catholic and non-Cath-
olic readers alike, Greene was awarded a number
of specific honors, including Honorary Associate of
the American Academy of Arts and Letters in 1961;
an honorary doctorate of letters from Cambridge
University in 1962; Honorary Fellow from Balliol
College, Oxford, in 1963; Companion of Honour in
1966; an honorary doctorate of letters from Edinburgh University in 1967; the Shakespeare Prize in
Hamburg in 1968; and the Chevalier de la Légion
d'Honneur in 1969.

During the 1950s and 1960s the number of
books and articles about Greene increased significantly, peaking in the late sixties. His novels and
entertainments proved to have an unusually broad
appeal. They were enjoyed by the general public

as well as by demanding critics and university pro-
fessors. The fact that most of his novels were made
into films obviously extended their popularity into
quarters not available to most authors. Greene was
becoming an institution, and his books were en-
shrined in reading lists of thousands of high schools,
colleges, and universities.

Greene's several trips to Papa Doc Duvalier's
Haiti in the 1950s and then, for the last time in 1963,
led to his next novel, *The Comedians*. As Greene
wrote, "Haiti really was the bad dream of the newspaper headlines." The fears that he experienced in
Haiti in 1963, "the most critical year of Papa Doc's
rule and perhaps the cruelest," as he wrote, are
richly conveyed in the characters of this novel. After
the book was published Duvalier declared that it
was poorly written and had no value as literature or
journalism. Green reflected afterward, "If I had
known the way the President regarded me, my fears
would have seemed even more rational."

In 1971 Greene published his autobiography,
A Sort of Life, which extends only to the 1930s. The
book is redolent of a lost innocence stirred by the
memory of his childhood in Berkhamsted. If, as
Greene says, there is "a splinter of ice in the heart
of the writer," it derives from a profound sense of
betrayal of that idyllic childhood by the realities of
growing up in a flawed world. In 1980 he published
Ways of Escape, which continues the autobiography
for the next four decades. These two volumes are
very circumspect and reveal little about Greene's
personal life. Rather, they provide excellent mus-
ings on his own work, literary influences, politics,
and travel. To this day there is no significant biography of Greene.

The early 1970s Greene spent traveling to Ar-
gentina and Chile and writing *The Honorary Con-*

sul. After finishing that novel he began work on another, *The Human Factor*, a work based on the sensational defection to the Soviet Union of Kim Philby, Greene's old boss in the British secret service. With the publication of *The Human Factor* in 1978, Greene assumed that his writing days were finished. He was seventy-four years old. But, as he put it, "a writer's imagination, like the body, fights against all reason against death." Nine months after the appearance of *The Human Factor*, he conceived the idea for another story while he was having lunch in Switzerland with his daughter and his grandchildren. The idea turned into a short, bizarre novel called *Doctor Fischer of Geneva or the Bomb Party*, published in 1980. *Ways of Escape*, which appeared the same year, was perhaps Greene's attempt to tell his own story while he still had a chance to defend himself against future biographers.

For the past sixteen years Greene has lived separated from his wife as a semirecluse in a modest two-room apartment overlooking Antibes harbor. His quiet life there, however, was disrupted in 1982 by his involvement in a battle against the criminal underworld of the Côte d'Azur. It is a complicated story, worthy of his own fiction. When Greene was in the Belgian Congo in 1960 to research *A Burnt-Out Case*, he lived for a time with a French-Swiss couple named Jacques and Yvonne and their six-year-old daughter Martine. When he resettled in Antibes in 1966, he discovered that his old friends had moved nearby. Martine, of whom Greene was very fond, had married a local realtor named Daniel. The marriage was short-lived, and the divorce settlement, which awarded Yvonne custody of their child, Alexandra, was revoked after Daniel began new legal proceedings.

Greene's sympathy with Martine led him to look more deeply into Daniel's background. Daniel had supposedly told Martine that he had the "police in my pocket" and that he would call on his criminal connections if she tried to reclaim their daughter. As Greene probed more deeply into Daniel's criminal record, Daniel's former mistress warned Greene that Daniel planned to murder Martine's parents and Greene himself.

In order to gain public attention for what appeared to Greene to be government-sponsored injustice, he returned his Legion of Honor to the French government. He also wrote and published an account of the entire affair in a thirty-page pamphlet called *J'Accuse,* named after Zola's famous essay. This publication angered local authorities and businessmen because of its damaging effects on the tourist trade in Nice, and a series of legal battles have been set in motion against Greene by Daniel and government officials.

Greene's early interest in communism and Catholicism comes full circle in his most recent novel, *Monsignor Quixote* (1982). It is the story of a simple parish priest named Father Quixote who journeys across Spain in the company of his friend, Sancho Zancas, a communist ex-mayor of the village. The novel is essentially an extended dialogue between the two men as to the virtues and vices of Catholicism and communism. It is as if Greene's lifelong attraction to both "theologies" is finally debated and analyzed in his mind through these two human and richly comic personalities.

Despite his self-imposed exile in France, one wonders if Greene will ever be content until he returns to the place of his childhood, a symbolic realm he has sought in his travels and recreated in his fiction. As he himself reflects on Berkhamsted, he expresses a profound nostalgia: "I feel it would be strange if, through the workings of coincidence, through the unconscious sources of action, through folly or wisdom, I were not brought back to die there in the place where everything was born."

2

Novels

Graham Greene has been called a Manichaean, a Jansenist, a quietist, and an extentialist, and he has been taken to task for being an anti-American, a Catholic propagandist, a bad Catholic, a snob, a merely clever writer, a slanderer, and a political meddler. But he has never, to my knowledge, been called boring.

There are two main reasons why Greene is an exciting writer. First, he is a consummate storyteller who can spin out thrilling and suspenseful plots full of remarkable characters and colorful detail. Greene's "hated obsession of trying to make imaginary characters live" has given us some of the most varied and memorable characters in twentieth-century literature: Pinkie Brown, the teenaged killer in *Brighton Rock*; the nameless whisky priest in *The Power and the Glory*; the pity-stricken Scobie in *The Heart of the Matter*; the mysterious and sinister Harry Lime in *The Third Man*; the wonderfully comic James Wormwold in *Our Man in Havana*; Querry, the fugitive from civilization in *A Burnt-Out Case*; and Father Quixote, the saintly clown in *Monsignor Quixote*.

A second reason why Greene's fiction is exciting is that it offers a unique vision of the world, a vision derived from his obsession with certain

themes, characters, and events. Although it seems
obvious that Greene's obsessional compulsion has
its origin in his childhood, I shall leave this matter
to the psychoanalytical critics and biographers and
simply point out the forceful literary consequences
of the obsession. Greene is like Coleridge's Ancient
Mariner who burns with a constant passion to tell
the passersby his story, and like the Mariner he can
hold his audience with the hypnotic eye of a true
believer and weave his obsession into a compelling
fiction. As Greene himself put it, "Writing is a form
of therapy; sometimes I wonder how all those who
do not write, compose or paint can manage to escape
the madness, the melancholia, the panic fear which
is inherent in the human situation."

Although writing about the poet Walter de la
Mare, Greene accurately describes himself when he
says that "every creative writer . . . is a victim: a
man given over to an obsession." Greene's obsessions and fascinations are many and include innocence, evil, pity, hatred, the isolated and hunted
man, betrayal (the "Judas complex," as he calls it),
suicide, dreams, seedy and decadent surroundings
("Greeneland," as the critics name it), violence, car-
nal sexuality, and failure. His characters, as one
critic notes, tend to fall into four categories: the sin-
ner, the innocent, the pious person, and the hu-
manist.[1]

All of these obsessive figures, themes, and subjects are circumscribed by Greene's fatalistic and
pessimistic vision of the world. There is little
healthy humor or laughter in most of his novels, but
rather a sense of inevitable failure, pain, and suffering. There may be a God outside Greene's world,
but the focus is almost always on the twisted world
itself, its nightmarish oppression, its squalor, and its

seeming hopelessness. One critic sees as the ultimate motive of Greene's work an attempt to define
and objectify evil, to free it from the relativity of
values and abstractions—arbitrary justice, right and
wrong, good and bad.[2] Seán O'Faoláin, however,
puts the case this way: "All he can give to us is a
final hope, not intense, far from heartening, that our
immortal destiny may be greater than our mortal
desserts; but that we shall have small hope of release or even relief from the bondage of sin and the
devil here below, the whole burthen of his work
gloomily asserts."[3]

The novelist, however, is not primarily a
teacher or preacher or moral philosopher. He is first
and foremost an entertainer. Greene's Catholicism
and his obsessions supply much of the strength of
his novels. They are the muscles that make the body
of his fiction work, but they should not be viewed
in isolation from the total performance, which concerns itself with the human condition and the fundamental theme found in much great literature: the
struggle of innocence against evil and the hope of
redemption. The miracle that the entertainer performs in this instance is that after luring us through
episodes filled with suffering, violence, ugliness,
and evil, he makes us feel good. He appeals to our
profound urge to avenge an imperfect world that has
betrayed our own youthful fantasies and ideals. Allott and Farris best summarize Greene's motives
that touch our own: "The terror of life, a terror of
what experience can do to the individual, a terror
at predetermined corruption, is the motive force that
drives Greene as a novelist."[4]

Greene has divided his fiction into two groups,
novels and entertainments. He used the term "entertainments" to describe some of his fiction in

order, in his words, "To distinguish them from more serious novels." Although this is not a useful critical distinction in general, it is a practical and helpful way of dividing Greene's fiction for purposes of discussion. Most critics, for example, view his novels as his major works. Furthermore, the entertainments focus on plot, background, action, and melodrama. They are less concerned with character development and religious or moral issues than are the novels, and they are filled with improbable coincidences and events. Evelyn Waugh sees the distinction in metaphorical terms: the "novels" have been "baptized, held deep under the waters of life," whereas the 'entertainments' are "merely playing a part for the reader's amusement."[5] But both groups of fiction, as will be seen, present similar themes and characters. The distinction is simply one of degree of complexity. First, then, I shall discuss Greene's major novels.

Before examining what critics consider to be Greene's first major novel, *Brighton Rock*, I think it valuable to review three of his previous books: *The Man Within, It's a Battlefield*, and *England Made Me. The Man Within* is important simply because it is Greene's first published novel and because its success reinforced certain themes and subjects that he developed in later books. The second two novels need to be noted, especially *England Made Me*, because they have been underestimated by previous critics and are long overdue a reevaluation.

Writing in 1971, Greene said that the poetry of Robert Browning has "influenced my life more than any of the Beatitudes" and that if he were to choose an epigraph for all the novels he had ever written it would be the following lines from "Bishop Blougram's Apology":

> Our interest's on the dangerous edge of things.
> The honest thief, the tender murderer,
> The superstitious atheist, demi-rep
> That loves and saves her soul in new French books—
> We watch while those in equilibrium keep
> The giddy line midway.

Greene goes on to write that "With Robert Browning I lived in a region of adulteries, of assignations at dark street corners, of lascivious priests and hasty dagger thrusts, and of sexual passion far more heady than romatic love." The keen sense of danger and adventure and the fascination for the grotesque that the young Greene developed from reading Browning as a young man were to play a significant part in shaping the novels he was to write.

The epigraph for Greene's first published novel, *The Man Within*, is from Sir Thomas Browne and reads, "There's another man within me that's angry with me." The hero's bitterness over his unhappy childhood leads him to betray his friend, his lover, and "the man within." Because of this triple treachery, he commits suicide at the end of the novel. Greene's lifelong concern with the problem of good and evil, with the danger and excitement that arise out of moral dilemmas, is clearly demonstrated in this melodramatic early work, as is his preoccupation with betrayal and suicide. Although flawed by sentimentality and naiveté, this work proved to be a good apprentice piece, and Greene's next novel, *It's a Battlefield*, showed a marked maturity.

As its title suggests, *It's a Battlefield* depicts life as a warfare against the implacable injustice of society. The hero is Conrad Drover, whose brother Jim has been imprisoned for killing a policeman who threatened his wife during a communist rally.

Conrad wants to see justice done in his brother's case, but while trying to secure his reprieve, he seduces his sister-in-law, Milly. He is thus faced with the curious moral predicament of being a hypocrite who seeks social justice. The assistant commissioner of police, on the other hand, is unconcerned with questions of morality, justice, or politics; he conceives of his job as "simply to get the right man," and his chief anxiety is over his impending retirement. Surrogate, a communist intellectual, has only his abstract social cause in mind and wants Jim to be sacrificed so as to strengthen the communist opposition to the present government. Surrogate's relationship to Jim, however, is complicated by the fact that he is sleeping with Milly's sister.

Each character pursues the battle in his or her own way. Milly obtains the signature of the murdered policeman's wife on a petition drafted on behalf of her husband. Conrad buys a secondhand revolver and stalks the assistant commissioner, whom he sees as the symbol of all the injustice and pain surrounding him. But as he is about to shoot him, the rusty trigger jams, and a car screaming out of control runs Conrad down. He dies alone in a hospital shortly afterward, and the police discover that the revolver was loaded with blanks.

Meanwhile the government out of political motives grants Jim Drover a reprieve from execution, but the sentence of eighteen years in prison ironically proves to be a greater punishment than death, because it means his wife, whom he loves above all else, will be a middle-aged woman by the time he is released. As the prison chaplain says, "do you think any woman can be faithful for eighteen years to a man she sees once a month?" The final irony is spoken by the naive chaplain to the knowing assistant commissioner: "There's only one comfort:

he's got a brother. They're devoted to each other. He'll look after the wife."

One of the major points of this novel is expressed in the epigraph: "each separate gathering of English soldiery went on fighting its own little battle in happy and advantageous ignorance of the general state of the action." In their response to Jim Drover's imprisonment, the various characters in the novel reveal a complex mixture of motivations, ranging from intense self-interest to misguided idealism, with the end result being that justice happens, if at all, by chance. In this nightmare vision, Greene allows the chaplain's final reaction to represent the sane man's response to a mad world. The chaplain announces his resignation, because "I can't stand human justice any longer. Its arbitrariness. Its incomprehensibility." When the assistant commissioner asks if divine justice is not the same, the chaplain responds, "Perhaps. But one can't hand in a resignation to God."

In this grim wonderland the only way to survive is by flowing with the tide and by ignoring or forgetting the flotsam and jetsam. The assistant commissioner is such a survivor. Recognizing that the chaplain is right to resign, the assistant commissioner briefly considers the idea himself: "I am a coward, he told himself: I haven't the courage of my convictions; I am not indispensable to the Yard; it is the Yard which is indispensable to me. . . . If I had faith, he thought wryly; if I had any conviction that I was on the right side." But then, seconds later, "his spirits rose: all that worried him dropped away, like the little figures running back from the landing ground as an airship lifts." He forgets the chaplain, forgets Drover, and goes about writing up a routine report.

Those who fight the system and seek justice become victims of their obsessions compelled to take
desperate actions. For them there is no peace, and
they have no exit from their nightmare except death.
What contributes to the nightmarish absurdity of
Conrad's world is his awareness that "others had
made the rules by which he suffered; it was unfair
that they should leave him so alone and yet make
the rules which governed him. It was as if a man
marooned must still order his life according to the
regulations of his ship." In his frustration, guilt, and
anger, he strikes out against society like an adolescent. He buys a gun in the foolish and desperate
hope that he can murder injustice. No one, he believes, ever took him seriously as a chief clerk, as a
lover, or as a man ("that was the worst crime"). His
hatred becomes an obsession that must be released
before it victimizes him: "He was separated from
everyone he loved by his hatred. But when the shot
was fired and the man was dead, his hatred would
leave him." Finally, when he spots the assistant
commissioner and takes aim, "his hatred narrowed
to a stud in a man's shirt." Conrad's humanity is
similarly diminished by his obsession.

It's a Battlefield is one of Greene's darkest novels, marked by a strong social conscience. The people we see suffer are of the lower middle class. Jim
Drover is a bus driver and a communist and his
brother a clerk. Even though Greene was a Catholic
when he wrote the book, there is a complete absence of spiritual consolation or hope, and no sense
of a directing moral purpose in the world. One may
believe in values like justice, law, or love, but to do
so means inevitable frustration and cruel disappointment. Lust brings Milly's sister Kay fulfillment, but love brings Conrad, Jim, and Milly only
misery. This world without God and without pur-

pose accurately reflects Greene's vision of civilized society as hell.

Greene wrote, "I have always had a soft spot in my heart . . . for *England Made Me*," a novel that has as its subject, according to him, "a brother and sister in the confusion of incestuous love." Greene's attachment to the book is owing to his personal relationship to its hero, Anthony Farrant: "I was quite satisfied with my portrait of Anthony. Hadn't I lived with him closely over many years? He was an idealized portrait of my eldest brother, Herbert, and I myself shared many of Anthony's experiences." Because it was such an early novel (1935) it fell under the shadow of critically acclaimed works like *Brighton Rock* and *The Power and the Glory* a few years later. A few critics, however, have recognized *England Made me* to be among the finest novels Greene has written.

The story opens with a brilliantly evocative sentence: "She might have been waiting for her lover." Kate farrant is reunited in Sweden with her twin brother Anthony, after a long separation. Possessive and loving, needing to protect and mother him, she is never really happy without him. They are continually on the edge of discovery about their true feelings for each other, but both use their superficial sexual loves—Kate with Eric Krogh, the self-made business magnate, and Anthony with Lucia Davidge, an English tourist—to evade the real thing.

Anthony is the embodiment of "depraved innocence." He has "the round face that always looked as if only that day it had lost its freshness, like a worn child's." Thirty-three years old, Anthony irritates Kate, who felt "a man should grow up." But he carries his "absurd innocence" through a long series of seedy, disreputable confidence games over

the years. Incapable of holding a steady job, he has
been sacked over and over again, and yet makes
friends easily, protects himself in a cloud of self-
deception (proudly promoting himself by wearing
a Harrow tie), and comes through all of his shabby
experiences unscathed. In Kate's eyes "he was fear,
despair, disgrace. He was everything except success." Nevertheless, it is precisely because her
brother is "conceited with failure" that Kate feels
so drawn to him. In many ways he is like a cunning
child, charming, well-meaning, and without direction. Kate, on the other hand, has been successful,
and as the mistress of the powerful Krogh, she manages to get Anthony a job as Krogh's bodyguard.

Interspersed in the stream-of-consciousness reflections of Anthony are recurrent childhood memories of his meeting his sister in a barn. Later, together again just before he left her to go abroad for
the first time, "they were as open to each other as
they had been five years before in the darkness of
the barn." Greene deliberately leaves the details of
the critical encounter vague but clearly suggests a
tender, loving, and sexual relationship that later
amounts to a covenant between them. They happily
share the memory, never analyzing it or fully reach-
ing after its implications. But like a married pair,
Greene tells us, "they had as many memories in
common as an old couple celebrating their thirtieth
anniversary."

Unlike Anthony and Kate, Krogh fails to come
alive as a character. Greene himself acknowledges
this, and says that he is there only for the sake of
the story. He is a man of financial action who never
examines his feelings. He does not understand art
or poetry and feels exasperated when called upon
to make aesthetic judgments. Money is the only
measure he understands, and when his doorman

comments that a newly erected piece of modern statuary outside the office is "a bit odd," Krogh angrily snaps at him: "That statue is by Sweden's greatest sculptor. It's not the business of a door-keeper to understand it; it's his business to tell visitors that it's the work of, of—get the name from my secretary. . . . It's a work of art. Remember that." Surrounded by his modern steel and glass building, Krogh likes to be alone in the security of his knowledge that he deserves his success and that his credit rating is superior to that of the French government.

His comfort, however, is upset by the news that one of his workers, named Andersson, is planning a potentially crippling strike at three of Krogh's factories. Krogh is puzzled by the thought of having to talk to the troublemaker. He tries to think how Laurin, his lieutenant in these matters, who happens to be away, would talk to these men: "He had watched him often at his game. He made a joke and put them at their ease. I, too, Krogh thought, must make a joke. . . . I must enlarge my scope—the human side."

Krogh finally arranges to frame and dismiss Andersson, but Andersson's son, who "believed in the greatness of Krogh," but also believed in justice, comes to Stockholm to confront Krogh. Finding it difficult to get past Krogh's hirelings, Andersson meets Anthony (who says, "Been down and out myself"). Anthony exclaims angrily, "it's just about time he met one of his workmen," and gets Andersson into Krogh's presence. But Krogh's faithful protector, Hall, intervenes. He strikes Andersson on the jaw and kicks him in the stomach: "Hall felt no anger against him, no sympathy; only a deep unselfish love for Krogh which had no relation to the money he was paid."

Fred Hall appears only briefly in this novel, but his character is memorable. There was about him "an air of complete recklessness; his flat narrow skull had not room for anything but obedience to the man who paid him." He had been Krogh's dog-faithful protector for decades, and "he didn't trust anyone near Krogh except himself." His loyalty is admirable, but his recklessness is frightening. When flying back to Stockholm at Krogh's request, for example, we find him smoking in the plane's lavatory where "he spat out small perfect rings, endangering the lives of twelve passengers, a pilot, a wireless operator, and several thousand pounds of property. A little thing like that did not worry Fred Hall." It is hardly surprising, when Hall learns that Anthony has become a threat to Krogh by learning of Krogh's treatment of Andersson and his son and of a crooked financial transaction, that he murders Anthony by pushing him into a river.

The most fascinating character in the book is a shabby journalist named Minty. Minty's job consists of following Krogh around and writing up anything of seeming consequence he says or does. "He's News," Minty tells Anthony, "He's board and lodging to me . . . he's cigarettes and coffee." An Anglo-Catholic and English exile, Minty is a desperately lonely and sexually repressed figure. Once a year he organizes a gathering of Harrow graduates (unlike Anthony, Minty actually went to Harrow) in order to "keep in touch" and to enjoy "one evening in the year when one's not a foreigner." Anticipating Pinkie Brown's puritanical attitude toward the human body (in *Brighton Rock*), Minty finds the human figure ugly: "The body's shape, the running nose, excrement, the stupid postures of passion, these beat like a bird's heart in Minty's brain." This revulsion leads him to find even the Incarnation a sickening thought: it "was more to him than the agony in the garden, the despair upon the cross."

The central theme of the novel is that of the exile who seeks his home place—or something representing it—to put an end to his painful loneliness. All of the characters are in one way or another trapped or exiled. Anthony is in a rut that irrevocably leads to failure. He lives on the seedy edge of society unconsciously seeking the rebirth of his childhood innocence symbolized by his uninhibited encounter with Kate in the barn. Despite his worldwide travel, he always manages to recreate a sense of home, a sense of England, in the clubs of foreign capitals and at the old boys' dinners. Anthony "saw himself and Minty clearly as one person: the exile from his country and his class, the tramp whose workhouses were Shanghai, Aden, Singapore, the refuse of a changing world." When Anthony plans to quit his job at Krogh's and return to England to have "a relationship," as he calls it, with Lucia Davidge, Minty simply says, "I'll miss you . . . Everyone goes. Only Minty stays."

The most forceful image in the novel that conveys this sense of isolation and entrapment is that of the spider that Minty keeps under a glass in his bathroom: "A spider watched him under his tooth glass; it had been there five days. . . . He wondered how long it would live. He watched it and it watched him back with shaggy patience. It had lost a leg when he put the glass over it." Later on, Minty is directly compared to this spider as he lies in darkness: "like the spider patient behind his glass. And like the spider he withered, blown out no longer to meet contempt; his body stretched doggo in the attitude of death, he lay there humbly tempting God to lift the glass."

Anthony, Kate, Minty, the Anderssons, and Krogh all resemble the trapped spider. Their glass is a series of circumstances that overwhelm and circumscribe their freedom. If there is a God in their lives, he resembles a capricious tormenter, like the one Minty discovers in himself when he breaks the second leg off the spider when examining it, to see if it is dead or alive. He discovers that it was cunning and not death that had withered it. Although Minty and Anthony share a high degree of cunning, which has helped them both to survive, in the end, Minty's acceptance of his diminished stature and role in society allows him to outlive Anthony, whose restless and depraved innocence finally leads him to his greatest fear—death by water, a shabby baptism into the ultimate maturity. The only "religious" character in the novel, Minty holds desperately to "his fantastic belief" that, in dying, Anthony entered "some place of no pain, no failure, no sex." One recalls his earlier statement: "Everyone goes. Only Minty stays." Minty, the trapped and tormented spider. Even Kate, at the end of the novel, confides to Minty that she is going to leave the country, not for England, but, as he puts it, "I'm simply moving on. Like Anthony."

The only character to escape pain and suffering is Krogh, and that is because he never examines his feelings. He is like a business machine. Despite his varied background in Chicago and Barcelona, Krogh never developed a national sensibility like Anthony and Minty. He was "like a man without a passport, without a nationality, like a man who could speak only Esperanto." Ironically, however, Greene suggests through his imagery that Krogh, like Minty's spider, is also one of the trapped: "He was enclosed now by a double thickness of glass, the glass wall of the lift, the glass wall of the building."

Everyone, finally, is left deserted or betrayed. Anthony had planned to leave Kate for Lucia before he was murdered. Kate, of course, abandons the brutally insensitive team of Krogh and Hall, though she is worn beyond revenge and does not reveal their crooked business dealings. And Minty is left without his new and possibly last friend, Anthony: "This was the fourth friend. There wouldn't be many more." The novel ends with a list of Minty's pathetic belongings up in his room, his shabby, lonely future: "The missal in the cupboard, the Madonna, the spider withering under the glass, a home from home."

Greene got the idea for *Brighton Rock* from a newspaper account of a kidnapping of a man at Brighton in broad daylight. The gangsters in this novel who move in and out of this seaside resort and the local racetracks also have some prototypes in reality. The character of the gang leader, Colleoni, for example, is based on an actual hoodlum who, in Greene's words, "had retired by 1938 and lived a gracious Catholic life in one of the Brighton crescents." More important, however, than the literal newspaper accounts that provided some of the raw material for this story is Greene's fictional design that carries this detective story–thriller (initially labeled an "entertainment" but later changed by Greene to "novel") to a level of literary excellence seldom achieved in that genre. Greene reshaped the Brighton of childhood affection to create what he himself has properly called one of the best books he ever wrote.

Brighton Rock is the story of a seventeen-year-old brutal criminal named Pinkie Brown, who has recently assumed the leadership of a gang of racetrack hoodlums working out of Brighton. The book

opens with a compellingly suspenseful sentence:
"Hale knew, before he had been in Brighton three
hours, that they meant to murder him." An adver-
tising agent for the *Daily Messenger*, Hale is assigned to promote the newspaper at this popular
seaside resort. Because he had betrayed Kite, the
former leader of the gang now run by Pinkie, Hale
knows that the boy has recognized him and is planning revenge. The pursuit and murder of Hale are
set against a background of fun-seeking holiday
crowds, band music, flower gardens in bloom, and
a warm summer sun.

While seeking refuge from his killers, Hale enters a bar and meets Ida Arnold. Vulgar, sensual, a
little drunk, Ida represents hope to Hale, who stares
at her "as if he were gazing at life itself in the public
bar." He picks her up with the thought that "She
could save my life . . . if she let me stick to her."
Later, after she spends a moment in the lavatory to
freshen up, she discovers that her anxious companion has disappeared.

When Ida sees Hale's photograph in the newspaper next day with the statement that he died of a
heart attack, "her instincts told her there was something odd, something which didn't smell right." She
goes to his funeral and vows revenge: "Somebody
has made Fred unhappy, and somebody was going
to be made unhappy in turn."

Hale's job at Brighton was to distribute cards in
hidden places along his route as a promotional de-
vice for his newspaper. People who found the cards
were eligible for prizes. To establish their alibi after
strangling Hale (until his heart gave out), Pinkie has
Spicer, one of the gang, deposit Hale's cards. Pinkie
later goes into a rage when he correctly surmises
that Spicer was seen by a young waitress named
Rose when he slipped a card under a tablecloth at

Snow's restaurant—and that Rose would notice that Spicer did not resemble Hale's promotional photograph in the newspaper (the big prize awarded by the paper was for those who recognized Hale and challenged him for the money).

To cover his tracks, Pinkie befriends Rose and finally marries her, because he knows that a wife cannot testify against her husband in court. Meanwhile, Ida Arnold, delighting in her role as detective and avenger, begins to focus more clearly on her suspects, harasses Rose, and begins to frighten Pinkie with her insistent inquiries about Hale. Feeling he can no longer trust Spicer, Pinkie kills him by pushing him down a flight of stairs. He grows more paranoid and begins to mistrust others around him, including a member of his gang named Cubitt. After an argument with Pinkie, Cubitt offers his services to a rival gang, but they reject him. Shortly afterward, Ida discovers Cubitt drunk and frustrated, and presses him for information connecting Pinkie with Hale's death.

Pinkie begins to panic: "More than ever he had the sense that he was being driven further and deeper than he's ever meant to go." Pinkie's shabby lawyer, Mr. Prewitt, knows how Spicer died, and so Pinkie makes him leave the country for France. But Ida later informs Dallow, another one of Pinkie's men, that Prewitt was arrested for swindling before he left England and can expose Pinkie's murder of Spicer.

In a desperate attempt to rid himself of Rose, who has become an obsession in his mind of the horrors of sexuality and entrapment, Pinkie lures her into a suicide pact with himself. Before he sets off on his grim drive with Rose along the coast, he spots the ubiquitous Ida in a tearoom: "He looked across the tables; the woman's laughter was like de-

feat." He screams at Rose, "You saw her, didn't you?
Believe me—she's never going to leave go."

Although he initially planned to let Rose commit suicide—which she was willing to do out of
reckless love for him—and then escape, during the
final moments Dallow informs Pinkie that Prewitt
has been arrested and that there is no hope for them.
As he reaches for the bottle of vitriol, which he always carries with him, to hurl at Dallow, the acid
flies back into his face. He runs screaming over the
edge of an embankment and plunges to his death in
the water below.

The novel concludes on a note of terrible irony.
Rose's only consolations are the possibility that she
will have Pinkie's baby and the playing for the first
time of a gramophone recording that he had made
for her earlier on the Brighton pier. She had insisted
he make the record because, as she says, "one day
you might be away somewhere," and his voice
would be a comfort to her. After he makes the disc,
he tells her, "I put something on it—loving." His
actual message, however, was this: "God damn you,
you little bitch, why can't you go back home forever
and let me be?" The novel ends with Rose walking
toward her rooms in the hope that Pinkie's love for
her will be expressed and confirmed on the record:
"She walked rapidly in the thin June sunlight towards the worst horror of all."

Most critics identify *Brighton Rock* as Greene's
first specifically Catholic novel, but as David Pryce-
Jones has pointed out, "Given Greene's obsession
with the corruption of innocence, it only required
the imposition of concepts like grace and sin, salvation and damnation, to deck out an obsession as
a religion." [6] Writing about his young, evil characters Greene says that "the Pinkies are the real Peter
Pans—doomed to be juvenile for a lifetime. They

have something of a fallen angel about them, a morality which once belonged to another place." The outlaw of justice, he goes on to say, "always keeps in his heart the sense of justice outraged—his crimes have an excuse and yet he is pursued by the Others."

Pinkie Brown is the embodiment of depraved innocence, and his evil character is one of the most skillfully drawn in recent literature. Greene visualizes Pinkie in realistic detail, but his metaphorical language elevates the young killer's character almost to the level of a morality play or a parable. Early in the novel, for example, Greene describes Pinkie's eyes as "slate-grey" and "touched with the annihilating eternity from which he had come and to which he went." At the end of the story, after Pinkie's plunge into the water, we are told that "It was as if he'd been withdrawn suddenly by a hand out of any existence—past or present, whipped away into zero—nothing." On one level, Pinkie may be a common thug from Brighton in the 1930s, but on another he is a fallen angel, a tragicomic hero who, on an irrevocable course of self-destruction, transcends time and place.

Pinkie is a Roman Catholic who, like Minty, is revolted by sexuality. He looks at Rose "with his soured virginity" and remembers "the frightening weekly exercise of his parents which he watched from his single bed. . . . his virginity straightened in him like sex." He translates his sexual desire into violence: "Was there no escape—anywhere—for anyone? It was worth murdering a world." Ironically it is this very rage to escape, to strike back at the world, that destroys him in the end. When finally, out of sheer perversity, he has sexual intercourse with Rose prior to their marriage, he says, "'It's mortal sin,' getting what savour there was out

of innocence, trying to taste God in the mouth."
Rose is compared to God in the Eucharist, "in the
guts," and Pinkie takes satanic delight in the notion
that "God couldn't escape the evil mouth which
chose to eat its own damnation."

The theme of lost or betrayed innocence is central to this novel. The neighborhood in which Pinkie
was born and raised is called Paradise Piece and is
now reduced to rubble. The allusion to *Paradise
Lost* is appropriate but rather corny. Pinkie sees
some children playing in his old neighborhood, and
he hates them for taking his mind back to innocence.
But he knows that even these children are already
corrupted and that one has to go back a long way
further before he reaches innocence: "innocence
was a slobbering mouth, a toothless gum pulling at
the teats; perhaps not even that; innocence was the
ugly cry of birth." Pinkie's fear of sexuality is directly related to the theme of lost innocence. When
he realizes that he will soon be inextricably bound
to Rose as her husband, he feels as if he "were shut
out from an Eden of ignorance. On this side then
was nothing to look forward to but experience." And
experience, in Pinkie's eyes, is poverty, jail, worms,
cataracts, cancer, and childbirth: "It's dying
slowly."

Pinkie's only real choice in life is suicide. That
is his only way of escape from human contacts and
other people's emotions. Other people make Pinkie's world a hell, but at least he understands hell,
whereas heaven is just a word. As he says, "when
they christened me, the holy water didn't take. I
never howled the devil out." Later he proclaims,
"Credo in unum Satanum."

The last picture we see of Pinkie is one that
reflects the major themes. He runs screaming into
the water with his face steaming from the acid

burns: "it was as if the flames had literally got him and he shrank." This passage suggests the image of an infernal baptism "into zero—nothing." Greene describes his fallen angel here as a "schoolboy" doubled up like a fetus, screaming as he is "taken by a hand out of existence," almost as if he were being pulled out of the womb of time by a brutal metaphysical doctor.

Pinkie's girlfriend, Rose, is one of many of Greene's saintly females. Sixteen years old, a Roman Catholic, she complements Pinkie's evil nature and, ironically, feeds and supports it through her self-sacrificing and submissive actions and thoughts. Greene writes that "what was most evil in him needed her: it couldn't get along without goodness." Afraid of Pinkie at first, she quickly comes to love him to the point where she is willing to suffer death and damnation for his sake. To commit a mortal sin for Pinkie stirred in her both fear and pride.

Despite her youthfulness, Greene sets Rose on a higher level of spiritual awareness than Ida Arnold. When Ida exclaims to her, "I know the difference between Right and Wrong. They didn't teach you *that* at school," Rose doesn't answer but the narrator comments: "the woman was right: the two words meant nothing to her. Their taste was extinguished by stronger foods—Good and Evil." When confronting the implications of despair, "the sin without forgiveness" (Greene's favorite), Rose thinks: "He was going to damn himself, but she was going to show them that they couldn't damn him without damning her too. There was nothing he could do, she wouldn't do: she felt capable of sharing any murder . . . ; she wouldn't let him go into the darkness alone."

Rose's thoughts may represent an adolescent and melodramatic response to her situation, but unlike Ida Arnold, Rose has heroic potential. She loves Pinkie and is willing to sacrifice everything for him. As she protests to the priest, Ida ought to be damned for "Saying he [Pinkie] wanted to get rid of me. She doesn't know about love."

Rose is right. Ida lives primarily to enjoy the sensual pleasures of this world. Rose would die for Pinkie, but death shocked Ida because, as she says, "life was so important." Rose believes in heaven and hell, but Ida believes "only in ghosts, Ouija boards, tables which rapped and little inept voices speaking plaintively of flowers." She is the embodiment of a life force enjoying cheap port, sexuality, and any fun she can conjure up. Greene repeatedly calls attention to her "great open friendly breasts," suggesting both her unashamed sensuality and her nurturing womanhood.

The great irony of Ida's character, however, is that it brings death and misery. Greene says that "There was something dangerous and remorseless in her optimism." She seeks vengeance and reward because "They both were fun." The consequences of this fun include Spicer's death, Pinkie's suicide, and Rose's devastating misery. Greene clearly manipulates our attitude toward Ida by winning our sympathy for Pinkie and Rose. Ida is not, after all, a very convincing character, and even as a symbol of life and secular justice she is described so as to make us feel an uneasiness about her that sometimes mounts to disgust. We do not cheer when she finally gets her man. Despite her apparent virtues and the enormity of Pinkie's crimes, she is not his equal. In contrast with Rose's obsessive devotion to Pinkie, Ida's fidelity to Hale's memory can be extinguished by the padded pleasures of a bedroom whenever she chooses: "If somebody said to her then 'Fred Hale,' she would hardly have recognized the name." She is also made to seem physically repulsive in Greene's descriptions of her large gluey mouth: "Ida Arnold bit an eclair and the cream spurted between the large front teeth." Later she "sucked the chocolate between her teeth and smiled." Even her big breasts, we are told, "never suckled a child of her own," and Ida "felt a merciless compassion" toward Rose.

Her least sympathetic trait, however, is her self-righteous assurance that she knows right from wrong. Her friend Phil Corkery says, "you're so terribly certain about things, Ida. You go busting in . . . Oh, you mean well, but how do we know the reasons he [Pinkie] may have had. . . . 'And besides,' he accused her, 'you're only doing it because it's fun. Fred wasn't anyone you cared about.'" She asks Corkery, "What's the harm in that? I like doing what's right, that's all." But as her pursuit of Pinkie draws to a close, Ida "felt quite sorry it was all over now." Her self-serving ethic of having fun and doing what is right clearly turns her into a superficial and sometimes grotesque parody of the hound of heaven.

As in Greene's previous books, there is little hope in the fallen world represented in Brighton, where justice is administered at the edge of a razor blade wielded by gansters or by a coarse, self-righteous tart. Things might have been different. Pinkie, for example, once thought of becoming a priest, but fate bends his world in a dark direction. Greene suggests that society is a deterministic force that creates monsters as happily as it does saints. But even Pinkie is allotted a civilizing trait—"any music moved him." While watching a romantic film in which the actor sings, "You're mine. All mine," Pinkie begins to weep. He shuts his eyes to hold in his tears, but the music continues: "it was like a vision of release to an imprisoned man. . . . He felt constriction and saw—hopelessly out of reach—a limitless freedom." The only freedom, however, that Greene's dark vision of society allows for his eternal adolescent, fallen angel, depraved killer, is annihilation.

The Power and the Glory is one of the most powerful of Greene's major novels, and the one considered by most critics to be his finest. The story is based on his journey through Tabasco and Chiapas in 1938, when President Plutarco Elías Calles, in the name of revolution, was closing down the churches and exiling or murdering priests and practicing Catholics. In his journalistic account of his visit, *The Lawless Roads*, Greene describes characters and settings that reappear in the novel. In a sense, *The Lawless Roads* is the sketchbook for the novel. In both works he describes what he has called "the fiercest persecution of religion anywhere since the reign of Elizabeth."

The novel opens in an atmosphere of death and desolation: a blazing Mexican sun, dust, and buzzards perched along the rooftops. Death and the threat of death pervade the entire story as the revolutionary government, represented by the nameless lieutenant, mercilessly attempts to eradicate the traces of Catholicism, represented by the nameless whisky priest. The story resembles a parable enlivened with the techniques of a thriller and fleshed out with the artistry of a novel.

The opening scene presents the priest shabbily dressed as a layman drinking a brandy with Mr. Tench, an exiled English dentist. Tench is similar to the priest in that both are trapped and abandoned in an alien country. And like the priest, "Mr. Tench was used to pain. It was his profession." Tench, however, is a fatalist who accepts his miserable life. The priest, on the other hand, has heroic—even saintly—potential, though he, too, resigns himself to the twists of destiny. When he misses his boat, his chance to escape to a safe country, he says, "I am meant to miss it," and rides off on a mule to minister to a sick woman.

Although Greene places his alcoholic hero in an atmosphere of squalor in the opening chapter, he is careful to suggest, even at this early stage, that the priest has a primitive nobility. He may have prayed and tried to escape persecution, but "he was like the king of a West African tribe, the slave of his people, who may not even lie down in case the winds should fail."

In his continuous search for safety and food, the priest winds up hiding in the barn of Captain Fellows, an English banana planter. Coral Fellows, his thirteen-year-old daughter, has risked her family's safety and her own by sheltering the priest, but as Greene makes clear, Coral has the heroism of innocence: "Life hadn't got at her yet; she had the false air of impregnability." She proves to be one of Greene's most mysterious minor characters, as we will see later.

The priest then returns to the village of his original sin, the home of a woman named Maria by whom he had a daughter, Brigida. Because the lieutenant has been taking hostages from the villages in order to frighten the people into refusing to harbor the priest, everyone here is naturally troubled by the priest's arrival. Although he deeply loves his child, now seven years old, he sees in her face his own mortal sin looking back at him.

When the lieutenant arrives to take a hostage from this village, the priest (still unrecognized by

his pursuer) tries to turn himself in but the lieutenant seizes a younger man instead. After the police
leave, the priest turns on the villagers saying, "It's
your job—to give me up." Turned away by the people and disdained by Maria and Brigida, he travels
to another village where, at last, he finds his Judas
in the person of a grotesque half-caste, the mestizo,
whose face is distinguished by his two remaining
yellow teeth sticking out of either side of his mouth.

The two men travel together toward Carmen,
where the priest was born and where his parents
are buried. When the mestizo declares, "I wouldn't
betray you. I'm a Christian," the priest knows that
"He was in the presence of Judas." He eventually
leaves the half-caste behind and enters the town
alone, seeking some wine that he might say mass.
Shortly thereafter he is arrested by the police for
possessing brandy (liquor was outlawed by the
state) and thrown into jail. When he is later released,
the lieutenant, still unaware of who the prisoner is,
gives him some money.

Continuing his flight, the priest stops at the now
abandoned Fellows plantation and recalls how
much he had counted on Coral for his safety. He
remembers her readiness to swear revenge on anyone who hurt him, and then he remembers, by way
of contrast, his own daughter who had recently en-
ticed and rejected him. Driven by hunger, he fights
a mongrel dog for a bone, and then comes upon a
three-year-old child who has been shot and killed
by the police. To appease the grief-stricken mother
the priest puts a lump of sugar in the child's mouth
"in case a miracle should still happen."

The priest then crosses the mountains to freedom in a neighboring state, where he is taken in by
Mr. Lehr and his sister, German Americans who run
a mining operation. But this peaceful interlude is

soon interrupted when the mestizo reappears. He lures the priest back to Tabasco to hear the confession of an American murderer named James Calver, who has been fatally wounded by the police. The priest knows that he is walking into a trap, that the half-caste will now betray him, but his sense of priestly responsibility and his fatalism lead him toward his captors. The mestizo delivers the priest to the police and collects his reward.

Imprisoned and awaiting his execution for treason, the priest drinks his final brandies and prays for his daughter: "O God, help her. Damn me, I deserve it, but let her live forever." Shortly before he goes to his death, he has a dream in which Coral Fellows appears to serve him wine. She instructs him in Morse code, and he and a whole invisible congregation tap out a message, which she translates for him as meaning "news." As he goes before the firing squad. "He knew now that at the end there was only one thing that counted—to be a saint."

After the priest leaves the Fellows' barn, Coral's behavior changes. She begins wondering if there is a God and if there really was a virgin birth. Later, in the vacant barn she discovers some little crosses that the priest has chalked on the wall and "stood in pain and looked at them: a horrible novelty enclosed her whole morning: it was as if today everything was memorable." Her recognition of the meaning of suffering and spirituality coincides with her first menstrual period, suggesting her growth into an even more awesome world: "She was ready to accept any responsibility, even that of vengeance, without a second thought. It was her life." Ironically, it also proves to be her death. She apparently goes off and meets a violent end, but Greene never makes clear precisely what happened to her, thereby suggesting that her innocent spirit will prevail over the godless cruelty and decadence of the time.

Coral seems to represent for Greene a primitive innocence that has been touched and transformed by the priest, and she becomes a sort of ministering angel. She physically vanishes from the novel but inhabits the priest's thoughts and dreams, and comforts him in his last desperate moment. The "news" that she teaches him to tap out in code is possibly the Gospel itself, which will survive the government's persecution through the secret but enduring ministry of the church—represented by the priest, his successors, and the innocent children, like Coral Fellows, who will continue to harbor and comfort the exiled priests until the church is restored.

The final chapter of the novel shows the effect that the priest has had on some of the other characters. Captain and Mrs. Fellows are in a hotel room discussing their planned return home to England. Beneath the surface of their conversation is a devastating realization that their daughter's death has rendered their own lives empty and meaningless. Mrs. Fellows tells her husband not to bring up the subject: "But we agreed, dear, didn't we, that it was better just to say nothing at all, ever? We mustn't be morbid." Ironically, Mrs. Fellows is obsessed with the idea of death and wants to flee Mexico. She and her husband both feel abandoned now. "There's no one else," Mrs. Fellows complains, and the narrator comments that "they had both been deserted." The captain's last cryptic remark notes the effect the priest had on his daughter: "But the odd thing is—the way she went on afterwards—as if he'd told her things."

Mr. Tench, like Captain and Mrs. Fellows, feels abandoned, with no real hope of returning to his country. The sound of the firing squad turns his stomach, and after the execution of the priest, an appalling sense of loneliness comes over him. The priest could speak to him in English, knew his children, and Mr. Tench now "felt deserted."

One of the little boys in the town, Luis, who earlier admired the machismo of the lieutenant, now spits on him, the spittle landing on his revolver. A story about a Catholic martyr read to Luis by his mother triggers Luis's conversion, but this episode appears terribly contrived to force the point that the priest's death has a moral impact on the next generation.

The novel concludes with a mysterious stranger knocking at the door of Luis's home. He identifies himself as a priest, and Luis "put his lips to his hand before the other could give himself a name." The fugitive church, we are thus reassured, is still a vital presence and will survive the violence of oppression.

The theme of the hunted man establishes an exciting and nightmarish atmosphere to this novel that makes it a first-class thriller. But there is much more here than a simple manhunt. Greene has created characters who are human and symbolic at once. The priest and the lieutenant embody the extreme dualism in the human spirit: godliness versus godlessness, love versus hatred, spirituality versus materialism, concern for the individual versus concern for the state. After the lieutenant captures the priest, Greene provides an extended dialogue between these two nameless figures that forms a disputation which lies at the heart of his parable of good and evil.

When the lieutenant first sees a picture of the wanted priest, "A natural hatred as a between dog and dog" stirs in his bowels. His ambition to catch this man is a disinterested one. He has no personal animosity toward the priest but sees him as a symbol of the oppression of the Mexican poor, especially the children who, in his view, are corrupted by the church, and "He was quite prepared to make a massacre for their sakes." In short, he is a nihilist who wants to destroy the church along with the memories of his own unhappy childhood.

Even though the lieutenant is the antithesis of the priest, his obsession with the hunt and his dedication to his job of eradicating all traces of Catholicism from his land, lead him to live a life that is ironically priestlike. His simple lodgings, for example, are described as "comfortless as a prison or a monastic cell." Like the priest, he has an abiding concern for the children and the suffering poor but, unlike him, thinks the source of their misery is the church. The lieutenant is also said to have "something of a priest in his intent observant walk." Despite the openness, intimacy, and identity that develop between the two men, the priest has a more profound sense of love and retains the potential for a heroic action. The lieutenant, on the other hand, is a diminished figure at the end of the novel. For one thing, we are told, now that the obsession with the hunt has been satisfied, "He felt without a purpose, as if life had drained out of the world." And the child Luis, who earlier had admired him, now hates him, suggesting the lieutenant's and the state's failure to win the sympathy of the youth through violent social revolution. In the providential plan of the novel, the lieutenant's hunt for and persecution of the priest ironically turn the priest into a martyr in the eyes of people. The lieutenant hates the rich and loves the poor, he says, but he cannot understand or tolerate pain. He wants to let his heart speak "at the end of a gun," if necessary, to bring about a social utopia.

The priest, on the other hand, has endured pain, anxiety, and guilt for years, but recognizes in his suffering the purposeful presence of God's love: "It might even look like—hate. It would be enough to scare us—God's love." This philosophic insight is hard won. The priest is keenly aware of his weakness and failure both as a man and as a priest. An alcoholic, a scandalous priest with an illegitimate child, a man terrified of pain and death, he harbors no illusions about himself. It is, in fact, his self-knowledge that raises him to the level of the heroic. When he is in prison for possessing brandy, he tells one of the pious inmates who thinks he is a martyr, "My children, you must never think the holy martyrs are like me. . . . I am a whisky priest." But unlike old Padre José, who has married and accepted the life of a grotesque buffoon, mocked by the children, the whisky priest is redeemed in our eyes by his keen sense of responsibility for his sins and for the suffering he has brought upon others. His purgatory is in Mexico, in his years of flight, and especially in the rich torment of his own conscience.

He accepts his loss of peace in the belief that the only reason God denies him rest is so "that he could still be of use in saving a soul, his or another's." After he sees Brigida, his love and sense of responsibility for this child and her blighted innocence overwhelm him. A bastard with the hunted, alcoholic priest for a father, she appears to have lost her innocence prematurely and has little hope for joy in this world. Through her—and, ironically, through his sin out of which she was conceived—he finds his salvation. He knows that the love he feels for his daughter should encompass every soul in the world, but "all the fear and the wish to save [are] concentrated unjustly on the one child." His final recognition that sainthood is the Christian's

most important destiny suggests he has achieved a
sort of saintly martyrdom himself.

To be sure, he is a Greene saint, not a Saint
Francis or a Saint Anthony whose life shines in the
legends of selfless, charitable actions. Greene un-
dercuts any sentimentality in his hero. The daughter
he prays and dies for is doomed: "The world was
in her heart already, like the small spot of decay in
a fruit." And his final prayer is spoken with brandy
on his lips. But it is his humanity that Greene ap-
plauds here, in contrast with the abstract compulsion of the lieutenant "who cared only for things
like the state, the republic."

The lieutenant and the priest provide an interesting parallel to Pinkie and Rose of *Brighton Rock*.
Like Pinkie, the lieutenant has been raised a Catholic, depends on violence to solve problems, and
harbors a profound hatred for the world that robbed
him of his childhood. And like Pinkie, who needs
the goodness of Rose to complete himself, the lieutenant needs the priest to absorb his hatred and to
structure his life. The priest, on the other hand, resembles Rose: both of them are pursued, "captured"
by their evil counterparts, and driven to make a critical decision. Rose is freely willing to sacrifice her
life and risk damnation for Pinkie; and the priest
offers himself and his damnation to save Brigida. As
will be seen, this symbiotic relationship between
two characters is of fundamental importance to
Greene, and it reappears several times in his later
novels.

The Heart of the Matter, like *The Power and
the Glory*, is concerned with Catholicism, guilt, suffering, and death, but with an important difference.
Despite its human dimension, *The Power and the
Glory* conveys the quiet but overriding sense of a

parable. In *The Heart of the Matter*, on the other hand, there is, as one critic has noted, "an absolute integration of religious doctrine and human feeling."[7]

Major Scobie, the hero of this novel, is a middle-aged police officer in British West Africa. During his fifteen years of service he has acquired a comfortable sense of home and a reputation for unfailing integrity. His wife Louise is a nagging and restless woman who plans a holiday trip to South Africa to escape the languid, oppressive atmosphere of Sierra Leone and the embarrassment caused by her husband's failure to be promoted to commissioner. Scobie, whose love for her has long been replaced by an obsessive sense of pity and responsibility, borrows the money for her vacation from a Syrian smuggler and usurer named Yusef.

During his wife's absence Scobie falls in love with a nineteen-year-old girl named Helen Rolt, who has been widowed in a shipwreck off the coast. When Louise returns, Scobie still feels morally bound to live up to his private vow to see to it that she is always happy. Complicating matters further, Scobie writes Helen a letter to reassure her of his love: *"I love you more than myself, more than my wife, more than God I think."* He slides the letter under the door of her hut, but her native servant, who is in Yusef's employ, carries the paper to the corrupt Syrian. Yusef proceeds to blackmail Scobie by having him help to smuggle some diamonds aboard a ship in exchange for the damaging letter. "Scobie the Just," as he is known, thus entangles himself further in a web of lies. But far worse to him than his adultery, his lies, and his involvement with Yusef is the damning sacrilege that he is forced into by his dilemma.

After her return, Louise asks Scobie to go to Communion with her as a sign that "we've started again—in the right way." He goes to confession to Father Rank, but cannot bring himself to promise that he will not see Helen again and so cannot be absolved of his sins. In order to ward off any suspicion of his adultery, however, he receives Communion while in the state of mortal sin. He willingly risks eternal damnation rather than inflict pain on Louise. At the same time, his love and his sense of responsibility for Helen are so strong that he cannot bring himself to end the affair. Scobie makes a desperate offer to God at the Communion rail, one that is very similar to that of the whisky priest before his execution: "O God, I offer up my damnation to you. Take it. Use it for them."

Tormented by his religious hypocrisy and by the certain knowledge that his dilemma will lead him to inflict unnecessary pain on Louise or Helen, Scobie decides to commit suicide. Both women, he reasons, will forget him after his death and regain their happiness. He studies the symptoms of angina pectoris so that his death may appear to be natural, and poisons himself with tablets prescribed by the doctor for the pretended illness.

Scobie's death leaves Helen empty of feeling and of love, wishing she could believe in God, "as though perhaps after all there was one chance in a thousand that she was not alone." Louise, on the other hand, is left embittered and cynical. She learns of the full extent of her husband's affair and concludes that he was a "bad Catholic." Suspecting his death was a suicide, she is also horrified at the thought that he knowingly damned himself. Father Rank, however, holds out the possibility of hope through God's mercy: "The Church knows all the rules. But it doesn't know what goes on in a single human heart."

According to Greene, his intention in the novel was "to enlarge a theme which I had touched on in *The Ministry of Fear*, the disastrous effect on human beings of pity as distinct from compassion. . . . The character of Scobie was intended to show that pity can be the expression of an almost monstrous pride." But, as Greene notes, the effect on readers was quite different. They saw Scobie as a good man, a sympathetic figure tormented by his conscience and driven to his doom by the harshness of his wife. And in an attempt to deflate the numerous critical arguments on behalf of Scobie's salvation, Greene makes the point that "suicide was Scobie's inevitable end; the particular motive of his suicide, to save even God from himself, was the final twist of the screw of his inordinate pride." And thus, he concludes, Scobie should perhaps have been a subject for a cruel comedy rather than for tragedy.

The truth of Scobie's character seems to lie somewhere in between the views of Greene and those of his readers. Essentially Scobie is a sympathetic figure, demanding our pity and winning our respect. But he does possess, as Greene reminds us, a blind spot of pride that leads to his destruction. Ironically, however, we admire him for the remarkable consistency of conscience that he demonstrates throughout the story, even when this consistency brings him to the preposterous conclusion that his suicide will release God, along with Louise and Helen, from his painful presence: "You'll be able to forget me, God, for eternity."

Scobie is an attractively flawed human being. The soul of honesty during his fifteen years of police duty and a faithful, if long-suffering, husband for about as many years, he is in love with failure and imperfection. While others sneer at Louise and her taste for art and poetry, and shun her friendship, Scobie was "bound by the pathos of her unattractiveness." He protests to himself that "This is my doing. This is what I've made of her. She wasn't always like this." Shortly before he commits suicide this idea reasserts itself: "it was the hysterical woman who felt the world laughing behind her back that I loved. I love failure: I can't love success." He falls short of entreating her to "be disappointed, unattractive, be a failure so that I can love you once more." By that time, however, she has become too smug and cheerful in her righteousness to spark his nearly murdered feelings for her.

Scobie's love for Helen is similarly motivated. He always remembered how she was carried into his life on a stretcher at the dock grasping a stamp album with her eyes shut tight. Several months into his affair with her he begins to hear Louise's voice in Helen's arguments with him. He notices, too, that sometimes her face looked ugly, "with the temporary ugliness of a child." Her unattractiveness becomes "like handcuffs" on his wrists, and he acknowledges his possession by "the terrible promiscuous passion" of pity. He feels no responsibility toward the beautiful, the graceful, and the intelligent, for they can take care of themselves. Scobie's eye for pity is so finely tuned that, when he finds small misspellings in Helen's letters, his protective instincts are stirred and his sense of responsibility is heightened. Scobie's love for both Louise and Helen degenerates into pity and destroys his and their happiness even while he strives helplessly to maintain it.

The corruption of Scobie the Just is a gradual and irrevocable one brought about by his unyielding sense of responsibility and pity. He carries the seed of this corruption within himself—"pity smouldered like decay at his heart"—and all of his attempts to shield the women in his life from pain merely intensify their suffering and lead to his own destruction. The novel borders on the edge between comedy and tragedy in its relentless pursuit of this central irony. Scobie's actions bring down his world because he never realizes that his pity for others and his willingness to do almost anything to protect them derive, in fact, from selfish motives. Beneath the seeming self-sacrifice in his offer to damn himself in order to save Louise and Helen there is the sense of enormous self-importance mixed with cowardice. His pride is also seen in his patronizing belief that *he* made Louise into a social pariah and a nagging wife. Furthermore, he cannot conceive of either Louise or Helen living happily without him because, he says, they would always be wondering where he was, whom he was with, and what he was doing. The supreme irony of Scobie's pity is that it distorts love, decays his heart, and drives him to suicide. Helen is left a survivor for the second time. Louise, despite her bitterness at being deceived and abandoned, seems more concerned about the state of her husband's immortal soul than about her unhappiness. She is keenly aware of Scobie's inordinate pride, and when Father Rank suggests to her that Scobie really loved God, she replies, "He certainly loved no one else." Greene gives her the last word not merely to allow us to judge her bitterness but to put into perspective the irony of Scobie's pity, grown out of a fatal pride.

We feel sorry for Scobie because he cannot help himself. Watching his fall from grace is like watching the hero of a drama, who, flawed by a critical blindness in his character, seeks peace and happiness but ironically and irrevocably brings upon himself pain, suffering, and death. A conspiring world seems to close upon him at an ever increasing and breathless rate. If Scobie had received his promotion (which he is offered, ironically, shortly before his planned suicide), then Louise probably would not have gone away, he would not have had to borrow the money from Yusef, and he would not have been in a position to begin an affair with Helen. The novel conveys a strong sense of fatalism as a chain of interlocking events combines with Scobie's obsessive personality to diminish his freedom and finally make suicide the only means by which he can resolve his overwhelming dilemma.

Once he decides to take his own life, "the solemnity of the crime lay over his mind almost like happiness." Scobie's peace, however, appears short-lived, a few hours of calm before his death, because he believes he will suffer eternal torment in hell: "I've longed for peace and I'm never going to know peace again." It is impossible, in looking back, to lay the human blame for his tragic death on any one person. Louise, Helen, even Yusef, as well as the minor characters are all woven into the web of necessity by the promiscuous spider-passion of pity. The structure of the novel has the beautiful geometry of a web with all the lines drawn tight and with Scobie, the self-poisoned victim in its center.

In describing the last moments of Scobie's consciousness, Greene employs a haunting and ambiguous metaphor, which he had used earlier in *Brighton Rock*. As Pinkie and Rose drive out to the pier toward their final moment together, Pinkie is suddenly shaken by a powerful and strange sensation: "An enormous emotion beat on him; it was like something trying to get in; the pressure of gigantic wings against the glass. Dona nobis pacem." He withstands the pressure but thinks, "If the glass broke, if the beast—whatever it was—got in, God knows what it would do." Greene's own childhood fear of birds combines here with the image of the Holy Spirit as a bird to suggest that the terrifying presence that threatens Pinkie is possibly divine grace. Pinkie resisted it, as Greene tells us, but the case for Scobie is not so clear.

Scobie attempts to make an act of contrition for his sins, but the drugs begin to cloud his mind and he cannot remember what it is that he has to be sorry for. He then imagines that a storm has come up and that he hears someone outside the house calling him: "and all the time . . . outside the world that drummed like hammer blows within his ear, someone wandered, seeking to get in, someone appealing for help, someone in need of him." His last words are "Dear God, I love . . ." but he dies before he completes the sentence. Even in these last moments, then, Scobie continues to believe that someone desperately depends on him, but the language here is different from that of his earlier expressions of pity. Greene heightens the emotional tone as Scobie, dislocated by the overdose of the drug, fights with all his strength to reach the mysterious someone who calls him and who tries to enter the house. Does he imagine it to be Louise, Helen, his murdered servant Ali?

There is, of course, another possibility. Shortly before he takes the pills he carries on a dialogue in his mind with God. And God's voice, which speaks "from the cave of his body," pleads with Scobie to return to him: "I planted in you this longing for peace only so that one day I could satisfy your longing and watch your happiness. And now you push me away, you put me out of your reach." Scobie's aborted act of contrition and the possibility that "You" is the word missing from his last sentence

suggest his salvation—but merely suggest it. The
ending is ambiguous. As Father Rank says, the
church "doesn't know what goes on in a single
human heart," and one cannot, therefore, assume
that Scobie's suicide damns him to hell. In Scobie's
final minutes we are inclined to believe that this
tragic man, who has suffered deeply, will at last be
awarded the peace of God, but Greene appropriately denies us the restful certainty of that conclusion.

Captivated by the apparent ease with which
Charles Dickens used the first person narrator in
Great Expectations, Greene employed the same
point of view for his next novel, *The End of the
Affair*. Into this study of two passions—obsessive
love and obsessive hate—Greene also combines
techniques of the nineteenth-century and modern
novel, including the stream of consciousness (which
he first attempted in *England Made Me*), the diary,
the letter, the inner reverie, the flashback, and the
spiritual debate. Like *Brighton Rock* and *The Power
and the Glory*, the novel depicts opposing characters in a symbiotic relationship of hatred and love.
The narrator is an embittered man named Maurice Bendrix. A novelist, he studies the life of a senior
civil servant, Henry Miles, in preparation for his
next book. In the process of his investigation he falls
in love with Henry's wife, Sarah, and they carry on
an illicit affair for five years. The novel opens, however, many months after the conclusion of that affair,
with Maurice curious to discover the name of the
rival who appears to have displaced him. He meets
Henry, learns that he is about to hire a private detective to follow his wife, and arranges to handle the
investigation for Henry. He hires a man named Parkis—a wonderfully Dickensian character—who,

with the aid of his son, uncovers an exciting piece of evidence, Sarah's personal diary. The entire next section of the novel is given over to this diary, and we, like Maurice, discover the intimate thoughts and feelings of Greene's heroine saint.

Sarah's diary takes us back a year and a half to the last night she and Maurice made love. While they are in bed there is an air raid alert, and Maurice leaves Sarah to go downstairs. A bomb explodes, and Maurice lies unconscious beneath a door that has fallen on him. Sarah finds him, believes he is dead, and prays to a God in whom she no longer believes: "I'll give him up forever, only let him be alive with a chance." In an apparent miracle, Maurice returns to life, and she thinks: "now the agony of being without him starts," and wishes him dead again under the door.

At this point in the novel Sarah begins her painful spiritual struggle, one that takes her near the level of sainthood. The key word she uses to describe her life without Maurice and without a belief in God is "desert." "What can one build in the desert?" she asks, and "if one could believe in God, would he fill the desert?" She has made a solemn vow to give up her lover and honors that vow even though it was a pledge "to somebody I've never known, to somebody I don't really believe in."

In an attempt to free herself from the obligation of her vow, she begins to meet regularly with a rationalist preacher named Smythe who argues for the impossibility of God's existence. Ironically, however, he leads Sarah closer to God and to the Catholic church. As she says, "I had gone to him to rid me of a superstition, but every time I went his fanaticism fixed the superstition deeper." Smythe falls in love with Sarah and confides in her that his hatred of the idea of God derives from his hideous

birthmark. "Why should I love a God who gives a
child this?" he asks her. Out of compassion for his
pain, she closes her eyes and kisses the mark on his
cheek, thinking "I am kissing pain, and pain belongs to you as happiness never does."

By the end of her diary it becomes clear that
Sarah has achieved a kind of sainthood. Although
she still wants "ordinary corrupt human love," as
she says, she knows now that her vow has brought
her a new lover, God, and that he paradoxically man-
ifests his love through suffering.

Meanwhile, Maurice makes one last attempt to
win Sarah back. He discovers her sitting in an empty
church. Sick and in obvious pain, she begs him to
leave. Surprised by his pity and admiration for her,
Maurice observes: "when I began to write our story
down I thought I was writing a record of hate, but
somehow the hate has got mislaid, and all I know
is that in spite of her mistakes and her unreliability
she was better than most." Eight days later he learns
that she has died.

Maurice now turns his jealousy and hatred from
Henry Miles to God, his ultimate rival for Sarah: "It
was as if she were alive still," he complains, "in the
company of a lover she had preferred to me." The
next day he receives a letter she had written to him
shortly before she died, in which she says: "I believe there's a God—I believe the whole bag of
tricks. . . . I've caught belief like a disease. I've
fallen into belief like I fell in love. . . . Even though
I didn't know it at the time, I fought belief far longer
than I fought love, but I haven't any fight left."

In the wake of her death, Maurice learns of two
more apparent "miracles" for which she seems responsible. When Parkis's son became dangerously
ill, he prayed to Sarah Miles to help his boy. The
boy woke up the next morning without any pain or

fever and told the attending physician that Mrs.
Miles came and took away the pain by touching him
on the right side of his stomach. When he later meets
Smythe, Maurice discovers that his birthmark has
dwindled to a small blue patch. "It was done by
touch," Smythe explains. "Nobody treated my face.
It cleared up suddenly, in a night."

The more information Maurice uncovers about
Sarah, the stronger his hatred for God becomes. He
comes to see God as a devil who tempts human
beings to make a blind leap into faith. He cries out
to Sarah in his frustration, "All right, have it *your*
way. . . . I believe you live and that He exists, but
it will take more than your prayers to turn this hatred
of Him into love." Maurice cannot be cured like
Smythe and Parkis's boy because, as he says,
"Hatred is in my brain, not in my stomach or my
skin."

Maurice wrote at the beginning of his story that
it was to be a record of hate—of Henry, of Sarah,
and now of God himself. But by the end of the novel,
he has become an intimate friend of Henry, with
whom he shares a common grief, and his love for
Sarah has grown beyond physical lust and is now
intertwined with his jealousy of God and a growing
awarenss of life after death and the real possibility
that God exists and shapes his life. He ends his
story, therefore, with a prayer appropriate to one
who has been exhausted by a God who demonstrates his love by inflicting misery and suffering on
him: "O God, You've done enough, You've robbed
me of enough. I'm too tired and old to learn to love.
Leave me alone forever."

Greene introduces his novel through this epigraph, a quotation from the French Catholic novelist, Léon Bloy: "Man has places in his heart which
do not yet exist, and into them enters suffering in

order that they may have existence." And so, for
Sarah and Maurice, suffering brings about a spiritual growth. Through their frustrated human love for
each other they both move closer to God and wisdom. Sarah becomes a saint, and Maurice discovers
through his obsessive hatred and jealousy new places in his heart. His emotional and mental exhaus-
tion at the end of the novel suggests a surfeit of his
obsessions, and out of his world-weariness we assume he will, paradoxically, learn to love now that
he has experienced the end of the affair.

Unlike the terrifying, godless world of mere
chance and accident that Greene depicted in *It's a
Battlefield*, there is in this story a clear presence of
divine providence. Sarah expresses this important
theme in her diary: "He [Maurice] was on your side
all the time without knowing it too. He worked for
it with his anger and his jealousy, and he worked
for it with his love. For he gave me so much love
and I gave him so much love that soon there wasn't
anything left when we'd finished but You."

If God is a devil tempting one to leap, as Maurice says, then by the end of the story Maurice is only
a few inches from the frightening precipice. Sarah
has made the leap, and Maurice is persuaded that
if *she* is a saint, "it's not so difficult to be a saint."
The implication of his remark is that an ordinary
person, flawed by her passions and obsessions, is
capable of caring more about someone else than herself, and in the commitment to that self-sacrifice
achieves saintliness. The same might be said about
Greene's whisky priest, who recognizes that God's
love might easily be mistaken for hatred, who dies
in order to save the soul of his daughter and who in
the end realizes that sainthood is all that counts.

Writing about this novel years later, Greene
says it is the story "of a man who was to be driven

and overwhelmed by the accumulation of natural coincidences, until he broke and began to accept the incredible—the possibility of a God." Although Greene does not say so, it seems probable that he got the idea for the story from one of his favorite Browning poems, "Bishop Blougram's Apology." The bishop points out to a skeptic: "All we have gained then by our unbelief / Is a life of doubt diversified by faith, / For one of faith diversified by doubt." The nagging consideration for the doubter, he concludes, is "the grand Perhaps." The atheism of Maurice Bendrix is overwhelmed by a series of seeming coincidences—from his regaining of consciousness after the bomb explodes to his discovery of the cures of Smythe and the boy—until he is face to face with the terrible "grand Perhaps."

The Quiet American, set in Indochina during the time the French army was waging war with the Vietminh, has acquired a new relevance since it first appeared in 1955. Alden Pyle, Greene's "quiet American," anticipates the painful folly of the American intervention in Vietnam some years later.

The story is told from the point of view of Thomas Fowler, an English journalist, and opens shortly after Alden Pyle's mysterious death, with Fowler being questioned by a French inspector named Vigot. Fowler explains that Pyle worked for the Economic Aid mission, which secretly funneled money to a mysterious Third Force headed by General Thé, who planned to overthrow both the French army and the communist Vietminh. Fowler then gives Vigot a brief sketch of Pyle's character: "He's a good chap in his way. Serious. . . . A quiet American." He remembers Pyle's gangly legs, crew cut, and youthful gaze, which made him seem "incapable of harm." He was determined, Fowler goes on to say, "to do good, not to any individual person but to a country, a world." After giving to Vigot this rather ambiguous picture of the innocent Pyle, who was "good in his way," Fowler thinks to himself: "Not that Pyle was very important. It wouldn't have done to cable the details of his true career, that before he died he had been responsible for at least fifty deaths." The novel returns to Fowler's first meeting with Pyle, and we are treated to the full story of the bizarre relationship between these two men.

Through the characters of Pyle and Fowler, Greene explores two important themes: the destructive inadequacy of innocence and idealism in a fallen world, and the dangerous timidity of living an uncommitted life. As usual in Greene's novels, opposite characters are strongly attracted to each other. The experienced and detached Fowler becomes close friends with the dedicated idealist Pyle. In the course of this strange friendship, Pyle saves Fowler's life, steals his mistress, Phuong, and is finally betrayed by Fowler to the communists, who murder him.

At the outset Fowler clearly states his attitude toward the war and all of the political intrigue behind it: "I'm not involved. . . . It had been an article of my creed. . . . I wrote what I saw. I took no action—even an opinion is a kind of action." Pyle, on the other hand, "believed in being involved" and, according to Fowler, "They killed him because he was too innocent to live. He was young and ignorant and silly and he got involved."

When Fowler first meets Pyle, his instinct is to protect him, though he later realizes that there was a greater need to protect himself. "Innocence," he says, "is like a dumb leper who has lost his bell, wandering the world, meaning no harm." The first harm Pyle does is to fall in love with Phuong.

Despite Fowler's protest that he is not involved, his feelings towards Phuong show his strong commitment to her. Although his attraction to Phuong seems to be based on her willingness to satisfy his sexual needs, to serve him his opium pipe, and, in general, to be his childlike servant, she answers a more profound need in him for security, happiness, and peace. From childhood he never believed in permanence and yet longed for it: "Always I was afraid of losing happiness. This month, next year, Phuong would leave me." Fowler's wife in England is High Church and would never grant him a divorce, he thinks, and yet, because of Pyle's pressing offer to give Phuong security by marrying her, Fowler writes to his wife asking for a divorce. He tells Pyle that to lose Phuong will, for him, be "the beginning of death."

Although hardly as obsessive as Scobie, Fowler is moved by pity for the suffering innocents he sees around him, including Phuong. Like Scobie he is a married man who falls in love with a young girl whose vulnerability deeply affects him. And like Scobie, who always carries with him the image of his dead daughter, Fowler cannot erase from his mind the sight of a six-year-old boy killed by snipers in a narrow ditch: "he lay like an embryo in the womb with his bony knees drawn up." And later, after a bomb is set off in a Saigon square, he is sickened at the sight of a woman holding "what was left of her baby in her lap" and of a legless torso that still twitched like a chicken that has lost its head.

In establishing Fowler's deep need for Phuong and revealing the complexity of his feelings for her and the suffering of the innocent bystanders in an insane war, Greene carefully prepares the reader for

Fowler's decision finally to become involved and to act. Fowler learns that Pyle was involved in arranging for the bomb blast in the city square during the shopping hour, killing and maiming several people. Phuong had been warned to keep away, but Fowler remembers the carnage of the other innocents and confronts Pyle with the enormity of his act. But Pyle simply and naively explains that there was supposed to be a parade including a few military officers, the planned targets of the blast, and that he was unaware that the parade had been canceled.

This event becomes the turning point in Fowler's relationship with Pyle. Earlier Pyle had saved his life when Fowler was wounded in the leg, carrying him in his arms to safety. Fowler's fascination for the paradoxical innocence of Pyle continues to grow. He is a man guided in his ideal of democracy by the writings of York Harding, the author of several anticommunist books, such as *The Advance of Red China* and *The Role of the West*. The ideals preached by Harding and practiced by Pyle are impersonal, concerned with saving countries for democracy at the expense of the people who live there. Recognizing this, Fowler earlier rationalized that his own cynicism and experience of the world may be worse than Pyle's impersonal idealism and, with regard to Phuong's happiness, says: "Oh, I was right about the facts, but wasn't he perhaps a better man for a girl to spend her life with?"

Although Pyle's innocence continues to hold a powerful attraction for the seemingly jaded, uninvolved Fowler, the inhuman brutality of Pyle's idealism finally leads Fowler to decisive action. Pyle becomes for him at times a symbol of an entire nation. After he steals Phuong, Fowler thinks, "It was as though she were being taken away from me by a nation rather than by a man. Nothing that American could do was right." Fowler's growing involvement is sponsored not only by this personal loss but also by the bloodshed of the innocent victims caused by Pyle's support of the bandit, General Thé. Fowler goes to the communist leader Mr. Heng and declares, "He's got to be stopped." Fowler agrees to betray Pyle to Heng's men and reflects on the advice a friend had given him earlier: "One has to take sides. If one is to remain human." After he sends Pyle off to be murdered, Fowler feels that he has betrayed his own principles: "I had become as *engagé* as Pyle."

After Pyle's death, Phuong returns to Fowler, who has just received a letter from his wife granting him a divorce. The novel ends with Fowler's acknowledgment that "Everything had gone right with me since he had died." His only regret is that no one existed "to whom I could say I was sorry."

The situation at the end, however, is more complex than Fowler allows. His decision to become involved in order to stop further violence ironically brings with it a deep sense of remorse and guilt because, like the mestizo in *The Power and the Glory*, Fowler has betrayed a man and caused his death. His motives may have been shaped by his moral outrage, but at the same time they may also have been determined by self-advantage. After all, he recovers his mistress by having Pyle killed. With the letter from his wife, his tragicomic story ends with the prospects of marriage and the hopeless desire to confess.

Unlike the whisky priest and Scobie, Fowler does not believe in God and must live with his guilt for betraying Pyle. There is no one to forgive him. Furthermore, he does not even possess a belief in a transcendent idea, as did Pyle, and he envied Pyle that ability to believe, even though the object of that belief—York Harding's ideal democracy—was practically inhuman. When Pyle says to Fowler, "Nobody can go on living without some belief," Fowler simply replies, "I believe what I report." The trouble with what he reports, however, is that it is all transitory, and Fowler's deep longing for permanence is never fully satisfied. The closest he comes to finding that permanence and its accompanying sense of peace is in Phuong. But even she, as he now knows from experience, can be lost, and, what is almost as bad, she was won at the cost of treachery. In his godless world, Fowler can find no true peace.

The conclusion of the novel highlights the irony of Fowler's earlier conversation with a Catholic priest he meets in Phat Diem. He tells the priest that if he believed in any God, he would still hate the idea of confession, of exposing himself to another man. The priest replies lightly, "I expect you are a good man. I don't suppose you've ever had much to regret." The central irony of the novel is that both Fowler and Pyle are good men, but each possesses traits needed by the other in order to be complete. Pyle needs Fowler's moral sensitivity and experience, and Fowler needs Pyle's courage and belief. And so, these two characters are irrevocably drawn into a friendship that, in the absence of God's grace and hope, ends in betrayal, death, and remorse. On the other hand, Fowler's willingness to take action against violence and ignorance, inspired in large part by his revulsion at the aimless suffering of the innocent, is admirable and heroic.

During the years since he published *The Heart of the Matter*, Greene has acquired an international reputation as a Catholic novelist. That unsought acclaim, combined with his successful attempt at comedy in *Our Man in Havana*, his trip to the Belgian Congo, and his reading of Joseph Conrad's *Heart of Darkness* and Pierre Teilhard de Chardin's *The Phenomenon of Man*, helped to shape his next novel, *A Burnt-Out Case*, the most intriguing and compelling work of his career.

A Burnt-Out Case tells the story of Querry, a famous Catholic architect who, weary of success, Catholicism, and sex, abandons the applause and pleasures of his European peers and seeks asylum and anonymity in the Belgian Congo among the lepers and the priests who attend them. Like the lepers around him, Querry is one of the mutilated, except that his malady is spiritual and psychological rather than physical. The term "burnt-out case" refers to a leper whose disease has run its course: the victim is "cured" but left severely deformed. Dr. Colin, the atheistic doctor who runs the clinic, tells Querry that perhaps his spiritual mutilations have not gone far enough yet: "When a man comes here too late the disease has to burn itself out." In his journal Querry records his spiritual affliction: "A vocation is an act of love: it is not a profession. When desire is dead one cannot continue to make love. I've come to the end of desire and to the end of a vocation."

There are strong autobiographical ties between Querry and Greene, who notes in his autobiography that "Success is more dangerous than failure . . . and *The Heart of the Matter* was a success in the great vulgar sense of that term. There must have been something corrupt there, for the book appealed too often to weak elements in its readers. Never have I received so many letters from strangers—perhaps the majority of them from women and priests." Obsessed with the theme of failure in his previous novels, Greene now examines the perverse fruits of his

own success through the character of Querry. Like
Querry, who did not seek the reputation of a Catholic architect, Greene acknowledges that the last
title he aspired to was that of a Catholic author: "I
felt myself used and exhausted by the victims of
religion." Querry feels similarly used up, and even
hypocritical. He says to the journalist Parkinson,
"To build a church when you don't believe in a god
seems a little indecent, doesn't it?"

Critics of the novel see in it Greene's recantation of his faith, and Greene admits that he experienced some of the same moods as Querry "but
surely not necessarily with the same intensity," and
that "in some of Querry's reactions there are reactions of mine." Greene goes on to make an observation that helps to explain the peculiar believa-
bility of Querry's anguish: "I suppose the points
where an author is in agreement with his character
lend what force or warmth there is to the expression." The points of agreement in this novel appear
to be many and carry deeply felt, personal rever-
berations.

Querry can no more escape his success than can
Greene. A revolting character named Ryker, the
manager of a palm oil plantation, recognizes Querry
from an old *Time* magazine cover photograph and
proceeds to resurrect his celebrated past. A pious
Catholic, Ryker is married to a young and innocent
native girl named Marie. Ryker's chief fear is of losing his child bride, and so he tries to instill in her
the fear of God as a means of ensuring her fidelity
to him and her performance of her "married duties."
Brutally selfish and religiously sentimental, Ryker
pursues Querry's Catholic past with a compulsive
need to see him as a flashy, saintly hero, an image
that conveniently distracts Ryker from any serious

analysis of his faith, doubts, insecurity, or moral
cowardice.

Father Thomas, a young priest at the mission,
whose faith is weak and who is in need of encouragement, also insists on viewing Querry as a saint.
He needs to confide in Querry and says, "You won't
understand how much one needs, sometimes, to
have one's faith fortified by talking to a man who
believes." Father Thomas is a composite of the
many priests Greene had met who, as he notes in
his autobiography, "would spend hours in my only
armchair while they described their difficulties,
their perplexities, their desperation." Like Querry,
Greene felt totally unsuited to, if not hypocritical
in, the role of confessor to the clergy. Greene's personal discomfort echoes loudly through Querry's exasperation with Father Thomas's insistence that his
[Querry's] loss of faith is comparable to the *noche
oscura* of Saint John of the Cross: "it's in your own
mind, father. You are looking for faith and so I suppose you find it. But I'm not looking. I don't want
any of the things I've known and lost."

Querry is also the victim of a hack journalist
named Parkinson who, despite his subject's protest,
is determined to portray him as a Catholic saint, a
famous architect who abandoned his magnificent
European cathedrals to work with the lepers of the
Congo. Querry, a man with neither faith nor the ability to love, is described by Parkinson as another Al-
bert Schweitzer. In a published article he quotes
Ryker's young wife Marie saying that Querry is one
possessed of "a completely selfless love without the
barrier of colour or class. I have never known a man
more deeply instructed in faith."

Querry's sympathy for Marie and her abused
innocence finally leads to his death. Ryker mistak-
enly believes that she has been sleeping with

Querry and comes gunning for him. Querry begins
to realize that he is a character in a tragicomedy.
"What a grotesque situation it is," he says, "that this
should happen to me. The innocent adulterer.
That's not a bad title for a comedy." When Ryker
confronts him, Querry "made an odd awkward
sound which the doctor by now had learned to in-
terpret as a laugh, and Ryker fired twice." And so
the black comedy ends. Querry's last words are
"Laughing at myself" and "Absurd," fitting comments on his situation. Ryker is satisfied with the
justice of his actions and goes on to feel more important both to man and to God, while Querry's ultimate fate is left ambiguous. Dr. Colin remarks to
the father superior, "You can hardly say it was a
happy ending for Querry." The superior replies,
"Wasn't it? Surely he always wanted to go further."

Greene's fictional wastelands are inhabited by
the "pious surburbans." These ugly characters embody what he describes as "the piety of the educated, the established, who seem to own their
Roman Catholic image of God, who have ceased to
look for Him because they consider they have found
Him." Trained by the Jesuits for six years, Ryker is
Greene's most powerful representative of the smug,
arrogant, hypocritical Catholic. Querry, on the other
hand, as his very name suggests, is a man searching
for the riddle of his own existence, a search termi-
nated only by Ryker's bullets. Unlike previous
Greene heroes, however, he does not contemplate
suicide. Rather, he rejects the values of a European
civilization that enshrines success while tacitly en-
couraging hypocrisy and corruption. Instead of
death he seeks the land of childhood innocence,
symbolized by Africa. Like Charles Marlow in *The
Heart of Darkness*, Querry reverts to a primitive
world in the hope that he will come to understand

himself there and find peace. But his Garden of Eden turns out to be infested with the likes of Ryker and Parkinson, European emissaries who have brought corruption even to this remote corner of the world.

The main theme of this novel is Querry's search for peace and innocent, spontaneous joy. This theme is carefully paralleled by the search of Querry's servant, Deo Gratias, for Pendélé. One day his servant mysteriously disappears into the forest, and Querry, who has grown very fond of the man, sets out to find him. Overcoming a number of difficulties, Querry finally discovers the poor leper in a shallow marsh, half in the water and half out, and remains with him during the night comforting him. The only sound Deo Gratias utters is the mysterious word "Pendélé."

Deo Gratis, it turns out, was seeking the same thing as Querry. Feeling that "there wasn't enough air" and that "he wanted to dance and shout and run and sing," Deo Gratias set out to find Pendélé, a magical place somewhere in the forest, near water. He remembered that he had been taken there once by his mother when he was a child, and he recalled "how there had been singing and dancing and games and prayers." Free then from his crippling mutilations and secure in his mother's affection, Deo Gratias reflects, *"Nous étions heureux."* Like the leper who has fabled a place where he is young, free from his disease, close to life-giving water and vegetation, and at one with unspoiled nature, so, too, does Querry mythologize the Congo as an Edenic sanctuary. Later, however, he admits to Dr. Colin: "It looks as though I shall get no nearer to Pendélé than Deo Gratias."

The father superior takes a cynical attitude toward Pendélé. He tells Querry that "People have to grow up. We are called to more complicated things than that." Querry's reponse is to recall the biblical counsel that we are "to be as little children if we are to inherit. . . . We've grown up rather badly. The complications have become too complex. We should have stopped with the amoeba—no, long before that with the silicates. If your god wanted an adult world he should have given us an adult brain."

As we have pointed out, before he wrote this novel, Greene had read and was much impressed by Teilhard de Chardin's *The Phenomenon of Man*, which argues for a teleological view of the universe: all evolution is moving toward the Omega Point, wherein God's creation will become one with him. Querry strongly resists this evolutionary flow toward a spiritual essence. Nevertheless, Greene wrote of his hero that he ultimately cannot evade God's will: he is among those "in whom reason is stronger than will, they feel themselves caught in the grip of reason and hauled along in their own despite, and they fall into despair, and because of their despair they deny, and God reveals Himself in them, affirming Himself by their very denial of Him."

While not crystal clear in the novel itself, this paradoxical theme is implicit throughout Querry's search for the peace of childhood and in the father superior's remarks that Querry's ending may have been a happy one and that "Surely he always wanted to go a bit further." Querry finally achieves the peace that was denied him in both Europe and Africa. In this sense, Ryker's intervention seems almost providential. Pendélé is not to be found in this world, and to seek it here can lead only to a painfully comic conclusion. Moments before Ryker's bullets strike him, Querry appears to realize that true peace lies elsewhere, and he has the last sardonic laugh.

Greene visited Haiti a total of three times before completing his next novel, *The Comedians*. Each visit brought him closer to the oppressive reality of François Duvalier's dictatorship, with its henchmen (the Tontons Macoute), the personal searches, the roadblocks, and the rebels in the hills. It is within this atmosphere of Haitian terror and violence that Greene measures the humanity of his major characters. "The hero Brown," Greene wrote, "happens to be a Catholic: it was this formation that made him the type of person he was; and Brown, as I said in the preface to the novel, is not Greene, even though Greene is a Catholic and the story is told in the first person. *The Comedians* is essentially a political novel."

On board a ship named *Medea* (suggesting tragedy) bound for Haiti Brown meets a "Major" Jones, who claims an adventurous and heroic war record, and an American named Smith, who, in 1948, ran for the American presidency on the vegetarian ticket and who, with his wife, is on a goodwill mission. The improbable meeting of these three men, who possess undistinguished common names "like comic masks in a farce," sets the stage for their subsequent humiliation and abuse by the Haitian government.

Brown is returning to Haiti to look after his hotel, now empty since the tourists have all been frightened away, and to continue his adulterous affair with Martha, the young German wife of a Latin American diplomat. Motivated by "a great love for coloured people," the Smiths plan to save the souls of the Haitian poor by opening a vegetarian center. Jones's mission is mysterious but turns out to involve a financial swindle of government funds.

When Brown arrives at his hotel, he discovers
in the swimming pool the corpse of the secretary for
social welfare, Dr. Philipot, who has slashed his
wrists and throat to avoid arrest by the Tontons Macoute. From this point on, Brown becomes increas-
ingly, if reluctantly, involved in the dangerous politics of the country. After the police assault Brown
and Smith for attempting to transport the body to a
cemetery, Brown agrees to collaborate with the
nephew of the dead Philipot, a poet turned rebel
who leads a small group of ineffectual guerrillas.
Included among these pathetic idealists is Joseph,
Brown's loyal servant for many years, who is crip-
pled from an encounter with the Tontons Macoute.
The police, meanwhile, discover that Jones is party
to a swindle of large sums of money, and come to
arrest him, but Brown takes him to the home of Martha's husband, Ambassador Piñeda, for asylum.

During his seclusion, Jones and Martha become
close friends, and Brown grows jealous, believing
that the two are having an affair. He encourages
Jones to live up to his military dreams by joining
the rebel forces, and together they travel to Les
Cayes. As they approach their dangerous rendez-
vous, Jones confesses that he has never touched
Martha and that his stories about a heroic past are
all lies. He was, in fact, rejected by the military for
having flat feet. Stunned by the absurd comedy of
the situation, Brown asks, "Why the hell are we
here, then?" Jones replies, "I boasted a bit too
much, didn't I?"

Captain Concasseur (whose name means
"crusher"), the head of the police, learns of the
meeting and confronts Brown and Jones. Philipot
and Joseph, however, shoot and kill both the captain
and his chauffeur and take Jones with them off to
the interior. Brown goes on alone to Santo Domingo

where he later sees Philipot and the remnants of his rebel group being led by Dominican soldiers into the city. Brown sees the body of Joseph carried on a stretcher and learns that Jones was also killed ("his feet gave out"). The remaining rebels, exhausted and out of ammunition, retreated to the Dominican Republic.

Brown happens to meet Martha here, and in their last encounter she tells him that his old confidant, Dr. Magiot, has been murdered for his communist beliefs. When Brown later returns to his room he discovers a letter from Magiot, which reads in part: "I implore you . . . if you have abandoned one faith [Catholicism], do not abandon all faith. There is always an alternative to the faith we lose. Or is it the same faith under another mask?" Having lost his faith years ago, and now having lost his friends, his devoted servant, and his mistress, Brown is reassured that he, like the others, are characters in a mad comedy. He thus remains in Santo Domingo to become a junior partner in a funeral business. The Smiths also settle here to try to establish their vegetarian center, but subsequent violence, Brown tells us, favors his business over theirs.

The central theme of this novel is that life is a comedy—a dark comedy, to be sure—and that all of the principal characters are playing parts forced on them by circumstance or acting out roles to disguise their true natures. Brown believes that one must choose the part one wishes to play in life but be willing to exchange it for another if the occasion demands. His mother, whom he remembers as "an accomplished comedian" and who inadvertently involved him in this Haitian nightmare by bequeathing her hotel to him, once told him that "As long as we pretend, we escape." And her final words to him were "You really are a son of mine. What part

are you playing now?" Throughout the novel he assumes several comic roles, including that of a seedy
hotel keeper, a lover in an adulterous affair, "the
part of an Englishman concerned over the fate of a
fellow-countryman [Jones]," and an undertaker.
When he was a young man, educated by the Jesuits,
Brown had faith in the Christian God and believed
that life was a very serious affair. The experienced
Brown, however, acknowledges that "it was only my
sense of humour that enabled me sometimes to believe in Him. Life was a comedy, not the tragedy
for which I had been prepared." He now sees God
as an "authoritative practical joker" who has driven
all the characters aboard ship with him "towards the
extreme point of comedy."

Jones, the con artist, is an exemplary comedian.
He not only assumes various guises throughout the
novel, but he is funny in himself and can make people laugh. He underscores the farcical nature of life
in this death-trap society by disguising himself as a
Haitian matron in order to slip past the police and
obtain asylum at Piñeda's embassy. Almost everyone—from Martha to Philipot's rebels—enjoys
Jones's company because, as they say, "He made us
laugh." In a world where the nightmare of terror is
the reality, laughter is a cherished experience.

The comedic theme is closely related to the
theme of commitment. Martha is devoted to her
young son, Angel. Dr. Magiot believes deeply in the
economic laws of communism. The Smiths are dedicated to helping the poor through their vegetari-
anism. Joseph is both a devout Catholic and a believer in the powers of voodoo rituals. Like Fowler
in *The Quiet American*, Brown is proud of his un-
involvement. Magiot reminds Brown that Catholicism and communism have one thing in common:
"They have not stood aside, like an established soci-

ety, and been indifferent." And when Brown and
Smith first inquire about Jones's imprisonment,
Brown asks, "I wonder if we ought to involve ourselves any further?" Smith responds with pride,
"We *are* involved," leading Brown to reflect cyni-
cally: "I know he was thinking in the big terms I
could not recognize, like Mankind, Justice, the Pursuit of Happiness." Nevertheless, Brown, like Fowler, has involvement thrust upon him, and he comes
to admire the people who are committed to an ideal.
After the Smiths stand up to the Haitian police, Mr.
Smith says, "Perhaps we seem rather comic figures
to you, Mr. Brown." "Not comic," Brown replies,
"heroic."

Brown's intervention on Jones's behalf, however, may stem simply from another assumed comic
role, rather than from any moral sense of responsibility. "I had left involvement behind me," he asserts, "in the College of Visitation. . . . Once I might
have taken a different direction, but it was too late
now. When I was a boy the Fathers of the Visitation
had told me that one test of a belief was this: that a
man was ready to die for it." Brown thus concludes
his comic story, still an unbeliever, uncommitted to
any ideal in a world that has crumbled around him.
His final role as an undertaker recalls Christ's judgment: "Let the dead bury their dead."

The Comedians marks a turning point in
Greene's style because it is the first novel to blur
the old distinction between novel and entertainment through its explicit comedic theme. His next
work, *Travels with My Aunt*, extends the comic
view of the novel even further. It is as if the madness
that Greene perceived in Vietnam in the 1950s has
now reappeared in the nightmarish horror created
by the Haitian government, a madness best dealt
with in terms of the comic and absurd, rather than

in those of the tragic and the moral. Life is serious
only when one believes that it has a purpose or that
one can do something about it, but when one's fate
lies in the hands of capricious and malevolent men
like Duvalier, then the element of dark comedy becomes a compelling factor in the novelist's vision.
God ceases to be a serious judge and becomes instead an "authoritative practical joker."

Greene does not succeed in presenting his dark
comedy nearly so well as he does his lighter comedy, as in *Our Man in Havana* and *Travels with My
Aunt.* For one thing, he repeats himself. The triangle of Brown, Martha, and Luis Piñeda is a weak
imitation of the more complex relationship that exists among Bendrix, Sarah, and Henry in *The End
of the Affair.* Brown is also a pale reflection of the
more introspective and sensitive character of
Thomas Fowler in *The Quiet American.* And the
figures of Mr. and Mrs. Smith are a simplistic parody
of American idealists already depicted in the character of Alden Pyle. Greene may be fascinated by
the peculiar innocence of Americans, but in this
novel he seems to delight in forcing them to un-
button their idealistic vestments so as to expose
their quivering, ordinary hatred. When Captain
Concasseur flourishes his revolver at Mrs. Smith,
the genteel crusader for racial equality screams at
him: "Get out of that chair, you black scum. Stand
up when you speak to me." She gains dignity in
Brown's (Greene's?) eyes only after "this echo of
Nashville racism had burnt her tongue." Like Pyle,
the Smiths are conceived as children in the bodies
of adults, American idealists playing with political
fire, the danger of which they never fully grasp.
Greene's anti-Americanism imposes a rigidity on
his usual craftsman's hand and leads him to portray
comic stereotypes instead of believable, rounded

characters. Incredibly, then, Greene expects the reader to believe that Brown learns to respect these foolish vegetarian missionaries as heroic innocents.

Even Greene's handling of the love scenes does not always ring true. In describing Brown's first sexual encounter (with a woman nearly twice his age) he writes: "Her fingers had no success, even her lips failed their office, when into the room suddently, from the port below the hill, flew a seagull." The bird proceeds to make itself at home, frightens the woman, and thereby renews the sexual vigor of the young boy: "suddenly I found myself as firm as a man and I took her with such ease and confidence it was as though we had been lovers for a long time." This sexual "resurrection," accomplished through the inspiration of a bird descending like the Holy Ghost on the sexually unbaptized, is romance turned farce. Even the language in this passage ("her lips failed their office") is inflated. Greene, nevertheless, must have relished the metaphor of the bird because later, when Brown lies impotent next to Martha, he muses, "suddenly I was back in the Hôtel de Paris and powerless, and no bird came to save me on white wings."

As the center of intelligence in this novel, Brown is a survivor because he follows his mother's advice: "As long as we pretend, we escape." Many of the committed people, such as Dr. Magiot, Dr. Philipot, and Joseph, do not escape, but rather die for their beliefs. Brown is not only flawed as a character by his lack of belief, but he is an artistic liability as a narrator. He has no soul or center of being with which the reader can relate: he is an actor, a chameleon. At least Fowler was driven to an understandable human act of betrayal that gave shape to his character. Brown, on the other hand, lives up to his drab name, untouched by the people around

him, a hollow man, spiritually and sexually dead,
who presides over a tale of meaningless cruelty and
comedy. It is indeed his job to bury the dead.

Travels with My Aunt is a hilarious account of
the adventures of Henry Pulling, a retired banker,
and his seventy-five-year old Aunt Augusta. Henry
meets his aunt—for the first time in over fifty
years—at his mother's funeral. Despite her age,
Aunt Augusta is a lusty, energetic, fun-loving
woman who tells Henry that "You must surrender
yourself first to extravagance" because "Poverty is
apt to strike suddenly like influenza." She has traveled widely, enjoyed numerous love affairs, and her
exuberance and zest for new adventures is so con-
tagious that Henry abandons his dull retirement (his
main interest in life being the cultivation of dahlias)
in order to travel with her to Brighton, Paris, Istan-
bul, and Paraguay. Their various escapades provide
Henry a unique education as he meets war crimi-
nals, a CIA agent and his hippie daughter, foreign
police officers, and two of his aunt's lovers, an African named Wordsworth, and an Italian scoundrel
called Mr. Visconti.

At the end of the novel Henry discovers that his
father was one of Aunt Augusta's early lovers and
that she is his mother. He also discovers that he
enjoys the excitement of his new life and chooses
to remain in Paraguay with her and Mr. Visconti
working for the latter's import-export business. The
story ends with Henry planning to marry the six-
teen-year-old daughter of the chief of customs, a
choice that reflects the worldly wisdom of his new-
found mother.

It is easy to misread this book as simply an account of the comic experiences of an old woman and
her dull, straitlaced "nephew." The narrative of this

picaresque novel is indeed entertaining in itself, but
there is more to it. For one thing, Greene deals with
the question of identity. As Henry gradually discovers his enjoyment of his aunt's life-style and
drifts away from the restraints bred into him by his
supposed mother ("your official mother was a
saint," Aunt Augusta tells him), he becomes a more
complicated and interesting person and the true son
of his free-spirited natural mother.

The major theme of the novel, however, is that
imaginative truth gives life its meaning and color.
Aunt Augusta is first and foremost a storyteller, like
Greene himself. Nearly a third of the book is devoted to her romantic tales of the past. With Mr.
Curran, who had to leave his job at the circus after
an elephant stepped on his toe, she founded the
"doggies' church" in Brighton. They baptized, married, but would not divorce dogs in their unique
church, which proved to be a profitable venture
until the police shut it down. Then she took up with
Uncle Jo, who asked her to find him a house with
three hundred and sixty-five rooms so that he could
live for a day and a night in each. Wanting to live
as long as possible, Jo only made it to the fifty-first
room and had a stroke on the way to the lavatory.
"He died on his travels," Aunt Augusta sympathetically concludes, "as he would have wished." Then
there are long accounts of her affairs with Wordsworth, Monsieur Dambreuse (a married man who
kept another mistress besides Augusta in the same
hotel), and Mr. Visconti, another rogue, who escaped from Rome during the Allied invasion by disguising himself as a monsignor, "even to the purple
socks."

All of these colorful characters, while actual
people whom Aunt Augusta has known, are richly
embellished and recreated through her skill as a sto-

ryteller. As Henry observes, "I thought of Curran
and Monsieur Dambreuse and Mr. Visconti—they
lived in my imagination as though she had actually
created them: even poor Uncle Jo struggling towards the lavatory. She was one of the life-givers."
Herein lies the heart of the novel. Aunt Augusta,
like Greene himself, is a "life-giver," a creative artist who gives meaning, energy, and form to the
chaos of experience. When she meets a woman
named Miss Patterson and learns that Henry's father
died in her arms, she becomes bitterly jealous and
treats the old woman cruelly. At first upset over this
confrontation, Henry recalls that he once read in a
book about Dickens "that an author must not be at-
tached to his characters, he must treat them without
mercy" because "In the act of creation there is always, it seems, an awful selfishness." Henry is
aware that Aunt Augusta creates her own world and
peoples it with characters loosely based on fact—
that she has, in fact, the compelling imagination of
a novelist. He learns that fact and fiction are inseparable but, as he asks, "What did the truth matter?
All characters once dead . . . tend to become fictions. . . . Jo Pulling [is] no less historical than Don
Quixote."

If Aunt Augusta performs the magic of a writer
who creates a world of believable people, then
Henry is the naive reader who falls under the spell
of that persuasive fiction, learns from it, and begins
to see through it to new depths in his own life. Aunt
Augusta, in short, educates him and expands the
scope of his imagination. At one point in the story
she leaves Henry behind in England, and he acknowledges that it was "as though I had borrowed
my aunt's vision and saw with her eyes" to where
"stretched another world—the world of Wordsworth and Curran and Monsieur Dambreuse and

Colonel Hakim and the mysterious Mr. Visconti. . . . To whom now could I apply for a visa to that land with my aunt gone?"

Aunt Augusta warns Henry that if he returns home and settles back into his old routines, death will be as close to him as the bedroom wall, "And you'll become more and more afraid of the wall because nothing can prevent you coming nearer and nearer to it every night." If, she continues, he chooses to live with her, "The wall will find you of its own accord without your help, and every day you live will seem to you a kind of victory."

And so, Henry Pulling chooses to remain with his creator—Aunt Augusta having literally given him life as well as having shaped his character (as a writer might have done). In sum, his decision to stay implies that he has at last discovered his identity both as her son and as a major character in the long and happy fiction of her life.

The Honorary Consul reverts to the dark comedy of *The Comedians* and shares with that novel a similar hero, theme, and setting. Greene, however, improves on the earlier work by writing from the omniscient point of view, thus allowing the reader the detachment necessary for understanding this comedy of human errors.

Set in a small Argentinean town, the novel opens with a farcical kidnapping that leads to a tragicomic story of betrayal, hope, and love. Led by Father Rivas, a group of revolutionaries, angered by the poverty, injustice, and corruption of their society, plan to kidnap the visiting American ambassador so as to bargain for the release of their imprisoned comrades. These ineffectual radicals ludicrously mistake Charley Fortnum, the British "honorary consul," for the American official and carry him off to their hideout in the barrios. Even after they learn of their blunder they remain determined to hold Fortnum hostage and threaten to kill him if their friends are not released from prison. In their naiveté, they fail to realize that the government has no interest in a mere honorary consul.

Doctor Eduardo Plarr, who is a friend of Father Rivas and the lover of Fortnum's wife Clara, intervenes on behalf of the unfortunate hostage. Like Brown in *The Comedians*, Plarr has lost his ability to believe and to love. Love "was a claim he wouldn't meet, a responsibility he would refuse to accept." He is, in fact, torn by his jealousy both of Fortnum's love for Clara and his son and of Father Rivas's belief in God. As Plarr syas, "I have reached a premature old age [he is thirty years old] when I no longer mock a man for his beliefs, however absurd. I can only envy them." Plarr's position as mediator is further complicated by the fact that he is the father of Clara's son.

The police finally attack the revolutionaries and fatally wound Plarr, Father Rivas, and Aquino. (Aquino is a more finely drawn version of Henri Philipot: he is a poet turned revolutionary and most of his poetry approrpiately deals with the subject of death.) The comic misunderstanding at the outset of the novel thus leads to the destruction of the radicals along with the ambiguous Plarr. Fortnum is reunited with his wife and son, and their mutual love is renewed. He decides to name his boy after Plarr because, as he says to Clara, "I loved Eduardo in a way. He was young enough to be my son." The fact that Clara once loved Plarr no longer disturbs Fortnum because now "Someone he loved would survive." His stay in "the anteroom of death" has sharpened his sense of life and hope.

As was the case with Brown, Plarr's parents are each of a different nationality, and he views his mother as a comedian: "Had she ever felt any love for his father or himself, or had she just played the comedy of love like Clara?" He also sees his mother as a decadent sensualist, reminiscent of Ida Arnold: "He wondered whether his father, if he were to walk into the tea room now, could possibly recognize the stout and pouchy woman who had a smear of cream at the corner of her mouth." His relationship with his mother affects his ability to love another woman, and thus "he had always tried to avoid that phrase of the theater, 'I love you.'" He loved his English father (who was killed while trying to escape from a Paraguayan prison) because he never used the word "love" or asked for anything. It is interesting that Plarr refers to Fortnum as "a man old enough to be my father," a phrase echoed by Fortnum later before he announces he will name his son Eduardo. Fortnum serves as a father figure for Plarr. Like his father, he is an imprisoned older man, one who asks for very little except the care of his son. Plarr's sexual possession of Clara, whose lovemaking he compares to his mother's, and his fathering of her child suggest a curious Oedipal relationship with Fortnum and his wife. Plarr can allow his surrogate father to die, but he envies his capability to love another person and therefore works to save him, rationalizing that he is doing so out of professional concern: "Doctor Plarr had a savage desire to tell him the whole truth. It was only the wounded body which stopped him. . . . To disturb a patient would be unprofessional."

Later, after Fortnum discovers the whole truth, Plarr outlines to Fortnum the comic nature of their plight: "It's not how I intended things. . . . Nothing is ever what we intend. They didn't mean to kidnap

you. I didn't mean to start the child. You would almost think there was a great joker somewhere who
likes to give a twist to things. Perhaps the dark side
of God has a sense of humor." Plarr wants "this comedy to end in comedy" because "none of us are
suited to tragedy." Like Brown, he acknowledges
that if there is a God, he is an authoritative practical
joker. But unlike Brown, Plarr pays for his involvement by losing his life. And when Father Rivas is
dying on a field next to Plarr and apologizes for caus-
ing so much suffering, Plarr whispers, "*Ego te ab-
solvo*," an absolution intended as a joke, "but he
was too tired and the laugh shriveled in his throat."
This playful allusion to Christ's forgiveness of his
tormenters nevertheless carries a grain of sincerity
and truth. Having rejected the foolish and sentimental gospel of Latin American machismo pro-
claimed by Saavedra, the Argentinean novelist,
Plarr exhibits a more difficult and authentic heroism, for he recognizes that "Poor drunken Charley
Fortnum wins the game." The game here is to find
a hope, a meaningful purpose in the comedy of life,
and Plarr fails to do so in failing to love or to believe
in anything or anyone: "I know how to fuck—I don't
know how to love," he confesses, but nevertheless
his intervention in the kidnapping and his subsequent death make it possible for Fortnum to survive
and to pass his love on to his son, something Plarr's
own father was unable to accomplish.

Unlike the cynical conclusion of *The Comedians, The Honorary Consul* ends on a note of hope.
Whereas the hollow Brown survives in the earlier
novel, here Fortnum, the pawn in the comedy of
politics, is the survivor, and his life gives meaning
to Plarr's death. *The Comedians* acknowledged only
the dark side of God, but in this novel Father Rivas
argues for the other face of God: "Every evil act of

ours strengthens His night side, and every good one
helps His day side. . . . we can be sure where evolution will end one day—it will end in a goodness
like Christ's." This echo of Teilhard de Chardin's
Phenomenon of Man marks the fundamental change
of tone in this novel from that of *The Comedians*,
and suggests that Greene now sees hope for his comedians and that love is the form hope must assume
to survive and to give the comic drama of life a shape
and a meaning.

Greene's next book, *The Human Factor*, makes
the compelling case that once a professional spy becomes emotionally involved with someone else "the
germ of corruption has entered his soul" and he is
lost. Maurice Castle has been in the employ of MI5
for thirty years and, like Kim Philby, after whom he
is modeled, has been secretly working for the Russians, but his love for his wife destroys his effec-
tiveness as a spy and sends him into his final torment.

"Uncle Remus" is a highly sensitive plan that
involves the United States and England in an attempt to control the uranium, gold, and diamond
interests in South Africa, thereby weakening the Soviet influence in that country. Castle's loyalities are
complicated by the fact that he is married to a South
African woman named Sarah, and he deeply loves
her and her son Sam. But he is also in the debt of
the communists because they helped her to escape
from her country and its racial laws. Now that he is
heading the secret service bureau for South Africa,
Castle hopes to undermine the repressive policies
of that government by leaking information about
"Uncle Remus" to the Russians.

As the novel opens, officials of MI5 are aware
of a leak in Castle's bureau. Sir John Hargreaves, a

country squire and head of the agency, calls in Colonel Daintry and Doctor Percival to ferret out the suspect. Daintry is a lonely man, separated from his wife and deeply concerned for the happiness of his daughter who is about to be married. Even though he is involved in the discovery of Castle's betrayal, Greene humanizes the character and allows a sympathy to develop between him and Castle: they are both family men, troubled by their domestic bonds. Doctor Percival, on the other hand, is an impulsive, cold-blooded professional, whose only extracurricular pleasure comes from fishing.

Suspicion quickly falls on Arthur Davis, Castle's young, lovesick, and careless assistant. In his haste to find the leak, Doctor Percival, on flimsy circumstantial evidence, concludes that it is Davis, and he poisons him in such a way as to make his death appear to be from natural causes. Later, when Castle tells Daintry that the wrong man was eliminated, the suspicion shifts to Castle, who is forced to flee to the Soviet Union, leaving behind his wife and child.

When Castle arrives in Moscow he discovers the irony of his work as a spy. His contact explains that the Soviets have a double agent in place in Moscow. This double agent passed back to the English all the material that Castle gave the Russians, thereby authenticating the double agent in the eyes of MI5 and allowing the Russians to pass on other information that they wanted the British to believe. Worse than this revelation that he was a mere pawn in the game of espionage, Castle senses that he will not be reunited with his family as promised.

Sixty-two years old, Castle longs for peace, for the quiet routine of family life: "To him it represented a security he had been afraid every hour he might lose." Now he feels he will lose it. Political and legal reasons make it impossible for Sarah and Sam to leave England. When Castle is finally allowed to telephone his wife, she explains her predicament and, trying to change the subject, asks if he has any friends in Moscow to alleviate his loneliness. He explains that an Englishman has invited him to his *dacha* when the spring comes: "'When the spring comes,' he repeated in a voice which she hardly recognized—it was the voice of an old man who couldn't count with certainty on any spring to come."

As the title of the novel makes clear, Greene is not interested in the mere perils and intrigues of the typical spy story, but rather in the humanity of his hero, his fears, desires, and hopes. Sarah's last words to him, perhaps unheard, are "Maurice, Maurice, please go on hoping." Like Brown, in *The Comedians*, Castle is a man "who left God behind in the school chapel" and who now sees himself as "born to be a half believer." And like Scobie and Querry, his main quest in life is for peace. Before falling asleep he thinks of his childhood hero, Allan Quatermain, "off on that long slow underground stream which bore him on toward the interior of the dark continent where he hoped that he might find a permanent home, in a city where he could be accepted as a citizen, as a citizen without any pledge of faith, not the City of God or Marx, but the city called Peace of Mind." Herein lies the central theme of the novel—the search for permanence and peace. The fact that Castle is a spy is incidental to this more important focus, a focus that links Castle to the earlier heroes Greene created, all of whom are seeking the same magical city.

Castle is a man without a country. A traitor to England, he can find no fulfillment in Moscow where he lives as an alien longing for another brief

moment of contentment with his wife and son. He
is left with little if any hope at the novel's end, despite Sarah's desperate encouragement that he not
despair (an encouragement reminiscent of Doctor
Magiot's plea to Brown not to give up his faith).
These fragile lifelines thrown out to drowning men
do not appear to be grasped. Castle's fate turns out
to be even more cruel that that of Greene's earlier
outcast, the whisky priest, another man without a
country who is painfully separated from his child.
The priest can at least offer up his life in the belief
that such a sacrifice may persuade God to protect
his daughter from harm. Castle, however, is
stranded in limbo, a half believer, with no control
over his diminishing future. He has failed as a spy
because he loves his family, and now his love proves
to be his greatest torment. The city called Peace of
Mind, which Greene allows most of his suffering
and driven heroes—Raven, Pinkie, the whisky
priest, Scobie, Querry, and Doctor Plarr—to enter
through death, is here closed to Castle. One assumes, of course, that as time goes on (outside the
novel), he will eventually be released from his anguish, but the fiction freezes him in a timeless and
exquisite moment of pain.

Under Greene's former classification of his
works, *Doctor Fischer of Geneva or the Bomb Party*
would be listed as an entertainment. In this short
piece of fiction, no character is fully developed, and
the central interest lies in the bizarre and sensational plot. Like the earlier thrillers, this melodramatic fable sets forth a hellish vision of human existence through its surrealistic action and setting,
coincidences, and exploding surprises.

The narrator of *Doctor Fischer* is Arthur Jones,
an Englishman who works as a translator and letter

writer for a chocolate factory in Vevey, Switzerland. He marries Anna-Luise, the daughter of the multi-millionaire Doctor Fischer. Jones opens his story with the intriguing statement, "I think that I used to detest Doctor Fischer more than any other man I have known just as I loved his daughter more than any other woman." The dynamic conflict between love and hate, which Greene first examined in *The End of the Affair*, is the established focus of the work. As Jones learns more about his father-in-law he is drawn by the man's demonic hatred into an exotic world of greed and death.

Through his invention of a toothpaste called Dentophil Bouquet (a comic extension of Greene's obsession with bad teeth, which he associates with decadence in several novels, but especially *The Power and the Glory*), Doctor Fischer has made a fortune that now enables him to wield godlike powers over an elite group of wealthy people whom he invites to his fabulous parties. Included among the "Toads," as Anna-Luise calls them, are an alcoholic film actor, a Divisionnaire (a high-ranking Swiss army officer), an international lawyer, a tax adviser, and an American woman with blue hair. This microcosm of the damned has substituted wealth and possessions for love and worships mammon in the person of Doctor Fischer. At the conclusion of each of his parties, the doctor presents his guests with spectacular gifts, but first they must endure outrageous humiliations from their host. As Doctor Fischer explains to Jones, "I want to discover . . . if the greed of our rich friends has any limit."

Greene's capitalists are seldom very believable characters, perhaps because of his unfamiliarity with actual industrialists or because of his hatred of what they represent. In any event, Doctor Fischer's character is an extension of that of Eric Krogh in

England Made Me. Both men are arrogant, isolated, power-hungry, incapable of appreciating art, and, most important, without the capacity to love. Doctor Fischer, however, exceeds Krogh's inhumanity through his conscious plan to humiliate and wound the people around him. Greene makes him into a symbolic character, one who identifies his greed with that of God. Doctor Fischer attributes his own cynical view of the world to God: "The world grows more and more miserable while he twists the endless screw, though he gives us presents—for a universal suicide would defeat his purpose—to alleviate the humiliations we suffer."

Doctor Fischer's own humiliation was to lose his wife to a common clerk named Steiner, someone who shared her love of music. The doctor fails to understand why she preferred Steiner's company to his, since he was "A clerk of Mr. Kips earning a minimum wage." Her betrayal of Doctor Fischer for a common worker damaged the doctor's pride to the point where he now lives solely to inflict his pain on others, and their willingness to suffer merely reinforces the contempt in which he holds all humanity. In retaliation for his wife's action, he has Steiner (who is employed by one of his Toads) fired and sees that he comes to ruin. Shortly after that, his wife disappears and, according to Anna-Luise, she is like an African who wills herself to die. Steiner claims to have seen Doctor Fischer cry at the funeral, which is the only sign of his wounded humanity revealed in the story.

Jones's happy marriage, meanwhile, comes to an abrupt end when Anna-Luise is killed in a skiing accident. Like Greene himself, Jones makes an abortive attempt at suicide, but then determines to go on living in order to humiliate Fischer for killing Anna-Luise's mother and for ruining Steiner. "I wanted to prick his pride," Jones says. "I wanted him to suffer as I was suffering." Like Maurice Bendrix, whose narration is characterized as a "record of hate," and who has lost his lover to a jealous God, Jones focuses all of his hatred on the godlike Doctor Fischer now that his "present" from Doctor Fischer, Anna-Luise, has been lost forever.

Doctor Fischer decides to give a final party, one that will test the limits of greed. As he explains to Jones the nature of his own insatiable and superior order of greed, he raises a Christmas cracker "rather as the priest at midnight Mass had raised the Host." This parodic gesture anticipates Doctor Fischer's death at the last supper party. Held out on the lawn of his estate at night and illuminated by a series of bonfires, this final party has the eerie atmosphere of a witches' Sabbath. There are six presents, one for each guest. Five of the presents are checks in the amount of two million francs each. The sixth one, Doctor Fischer explains, contains a bomb that will explode upon being opened. Greene's fascination in his youth with Russian roulette is thus re-created here on a grand scale.

Jones's great advantage at the party is his desire to die. Death would end his suffering, and his wanting to die undermines Doctor Fischer's sadistic game. When Jones's present turns out to be a check, his host taunts him for being disappointed. "You are just greedy for death. I'm not interested in that sort of greed." The last present, presumably the bomb, is left for the Divisionnaire, but he is too cowardly to open it. Jones, however, gives his check to the Divisionnaire in exchange for the present, opens it, and finds that there is no bomb. "Doctor Fischer had stolen my death and humiliated the Divisionnaire," thinks the dejected Jones.

Steiner then unexpectedly shows up at the party to confront Doctor Fischer with the murder of his wife: "She died because she didn't want to live. Without love." Doctor Fischer replies that "It was a disease I caught when you came into my life, Steiner. I should have told Kips to double your salary and I could have presented Anna with all the Mozart records she wanted. I could have bought you and her, like I bought all the others—except you, Jones. It's too late now to buy you." Doctor Fischer then walks off and shoots himself.

The man who held everyone in contempt fails to destroy the humanity of Steiner and Jones. Like figures in a Marxist fantasy, their poverty contributes to their salvation. Steiner's final judgment of Doctor Fischer is simply to pity him. As he says, "One can hate one man and leave it there. But when you begin to despise like Doctor Fischer, you end by despising all the world." And when Jones sees the crumpled body of his adversary, he notes that it now "had no more significance than a dead dog. This, I thought, was the bit of rubbish I had once compared in my mind with Jehovah and Satan."

Many years earlier Greene had discovered his fundamental sense of morality articulated in Marjorie Bowen's *The Viper of Milan*. Simply stated, it was that goodness has only once found a perfect incarnation in a human body and never will again. Evil, on the other hand, can always find a home there. And thus Raven, Pinkie, Harry Lime, Yusef, and Papa Doc roamed Greene's world. But his sense of incarnate evil changes in *Doctor Fischer*; his villain has become more insubstantial, and Greene's sense of the redemptive value of love has grown more keen. Pinkie's hatred lives on in the phonograph recording, and Papa Doc's cruelty outlives the timid humanity of Brown. But Doctor Fischer's hatred dies with him, and Jones discovers, upon seeing the doctor's corpse, the banality of evil, "the bit of rubbish" he once foolishly dignified with cosmic significance. It is as if Greene is revising his lesson from Bowen at last in order to acknowledge the mortality of evil and the immortality of love, a theme effectively understated in the denouement.

Throughout the book Greene plays with the notion that Doctor Fischer is Satan and that Jones is Christ, but it is only a suggestive and elusive allegory that he draws. Before he attends his first party, Jones is rebuked by his wife: "So you'll let him take you into a high place and show you all the kingdoms of the world." Jones replies, "I'm not Christ and he's not Satan, and I thought we'd agreed he was God Almighty, although I suppose to the damned God Almighty looks very like Satan." She grows angry and tells him to "go and be damned." But, because Jones and Steiner both possess the ability to love, they avoid damnation. The truth that Greene elicits from this bizarre fable is that love and a modest salary can save one's soul but that hate and wealth can destroy it.

In a perverse and secular sense Jones is able to save his life because he is willing to lose it. Doctor Fischer has no power over him because the only person he cares for is dead and gone. All of the Toads, on the other hand, live loveless lives and care only for their material acquisitions. Greene's Catholic-Marxist attitude toward great wealth and property thus finds expression in this fiction and echoes the exhortation of Christ: "Do not lay up for yourselves treasures on earth. . . . For where thy treasure is, there also will thy heart be." Jones learns to content himself with his warm memories of Anna-Luise, which he holds "like the relics of bone they keep in Catholic churches." He occa-

sionally joins Steiner for a cup of coffee and observes: "Our enemy is dead and our hate has died
with him, and we are left with our two very different
memories of love."

Out of the ashes of this black comedy, then,
arises Greene's growing insistence on the vitality of
love and its singular capability to give a meaningful
purpose and shape to an otherwise mad, cruel, and
tormented vision of life. But while the focus of this
work is on the embodiment of satanic hate and
greed, Greene carries on the dialectic in his next
novel with the incarnation of Christian charity and
poverty in the person of Father Quixote.

Greene's most recent novel, *Monsignor Quixote*, is a surprising capstone to his literary career.
This simple picaresque novel, modeled loosely after
Cervantes's masterpiece, exhibits the vintage
Greene. With a wisdom expressed through sympathy and humor, he turns away from the deadly ear-
nest treatment of his Catholicism and such obsessive subjects as pity, failure, suicide, and sex, and
creates a joyful comic fable of friendship, faith, and
love. Furthermore, in the dialogue between his
hero, Father Quixote, and his companion, Sancho
Zancas, Greene recapitulates and resolves his own
debate, extending through many of his previous
novels, about the relative merits of Catholicism and
communism.

Greene previously adopted the form of the picaresque novel in *Travels with My Aunt*, and, in fact,
compares Henry Pulling and Aunt Augusta to Cervantes's famous travelers. Henry declares, "I felt as
though I were being dragged at her heels on an absurd knight-errantry, like Sancho Panza at the heels
of Don Quixote, but in the cause of what she called
fun instead of chivalry." Furthermore, this novel

also anticipates the central theme of *Monsignor Quixote*—namely, that fiction may be a more powerful truth than historical fact. As Henry observes of his Aunt's colorful stories, "What did the truth matter? All characters once dead, if they continue to exist in memory at all, tend to become fictions. Hamlet is no less real now than Winston Churchill, and Jo Pulling [Henry's uncle] no less historical than Don Quixote."

Monsignor Quixote opens with its hero, a humble parish priest, Father Quixote, meeting the titular Bishop of Motopo, whose Mercedes has broken down on the outskirts of El Toboso. Father Quixote invites him home to dinner while the car is being repaired, but his housekeeper, Teresa, informs him that all they can afford to feed their distinguished guest is horsemeat and marsala. The "steak" is served and the bishop announces that he has never eaten a tastier meal. Some weeks later Father Quixote is surprisingly rewarded for his hospitality when the local bishop informs him that on the recommendation of the Bishop of Motopo the Pope has promoted him to the rank of monsignor. Father Quixote's bishop is so outraged, however, that this simpleminded village priest should be singled out for such elevation rather than the "more deserving priests in La Mancha," that he forces Father Quixote to take a "vacation" while he seeks an assignment for him in another diocese more befitting his new rank. The bishop dispatches a conservative young priest by the name of Father Herrera to look after El Toboso in Father Quixote's absence.

Meanwhile the communist mayor of the town suffers defeat in the election from "the forces of the Right," a loss applauded by the bishop, and the mayor decides to wash his hands of El Toboso and travel with Father Quixote across Spain. Mayor Enrique Zancas allows his friend to tease him with the name of Sancho, since Zancas was a surname of the original Sancho Panza. The two men set out for Madrid in Father Quixote's old car, a Seat 600, which he has named Rocinante after Don Quixote's loyal horse. As they head out of El Toboso the mayor inquires, "We must have something in common, father, or why do you go with me?" Father Quixote replies, "I suppose—friendship," and when the mayor asks if that is enough, he answers, "We shall find out in time." The novel attempts to answer that question, as their travels together lead them to perilous adventures through unchartered areas, both of the mind and body, and lead finally to a bond of love between the two men that transcends human friendship.

Given Father Quixote's belief that he is a descendant of Don Quixote, it is not surprising that he and his companion share with their fictional prototypes a number of similar experiences. The mayor insists on buying Father Quixote a pair of purple socks, a sign of his monsignor's rank, as a safeguard against arrest from the police, since the roads in Spain are still controlled as a result of the lingering influence of Franco's dictatorship. He even buys him a purple *pechera*, the bib a monsignor wears, and insists that Father Quixote wear it in an emergency. Thus armed, they set off for Madrid, drinking wine, eating cheese and sausage, and debating moral theology and Marxist doctrine.

When they arrive at Salamanca the worldly-wise mayor gets them safe lodging in a brothel that Father Quixote, in his innocence, assumes is a hotel. The priest remarks on the "large staff of charming women" and later blows up and explodes a condom he finds on his friend's nightstand, thinking it is a balloon. He apologizes for breaking the balloon, and the mayor tries to explain what a contraceptive is, but Father Quixote asks: "I don't understand. A contraceptive? But what can you do with a thing that size?" The mayor replies in exasperation, "It wouldn't have been that size if you hadn't blown it up."

In Valladolid Father Quixote continues his unorthodox ways by hearing a man's confession in a lavatory and by seeing a film called *A Maiden's Prayer*, which he assumed was a religious movie but was, in fact, a pornographic one. Confused by this, the first film he has ever seen, he has the production explained to him by his friend, but fails to understand how what the actors were simulating could be called love and confesses that he wanted to laugh but that the serious silence of the audience kept him from doing so. Late that night he is troubled by his failure to be tempted by sexual desires and prays: "O God, make me human, let me feel temptation. Save me from my indifference."

In depicting the cheerful chastity of his hero, Greene has come a long way from his earlier heroes' troubled sexuality: Anthony Farrant's incestuous love, Pinkie's perverted virginity, the whisky priest's lust, and the adultery of Scobie and Sarah Miles. Father Quixote is more like the innocent children of Greene's earlier work who, free from sexual constraints, express their love simply and directly and who do not experience guilt or anxiety in their relationships with others.

On their way to León, Father Quixote comes to the rescue of a robber pursued by the police. He hides him in the trunk of his car, he tells the Mayor, because "He asked me to help him. He said he was falsely accused and confused with another man." After they release him from the trunk, he demands at gunpoint Father Quixote's shoes, since his own are too rotten to allow him to continue his flight from the police. Father Quixote turns over his shoes and, after the man runs out of sight, observes that "If he had killed us the poor man would have been in really serious trouble." Having already prayed for "the poor man, Father Quixote heads for the cathedral explaining to the Mayor that he wants to thank God now "for *our* safety."

On their way out of León they stop to picnic on wine, their cheese and sausage having run out, become too drunk to drive on, and fall asleep. When the mayor awakens he discovers that Father Quixote has disappeared. It turns out that the bishop, infuriated by word of his priest's scandalous behavior, had Father Herrera bring him home to El Toboso. When Father Quixote realizes what has happened to him, he cries out, "Bugger the Bishop," and in saying that shocks himself almost as much as Father Herrera. The obscenity convinces the young priest that Father Quixote is not in his right mind. And, indeed, he is not. Both the bishop and Father Herrera, represent the rigid and doctrinaire aspects of Catholicism that constantly oppose and attempt to suppress the generous spirit of simple faith embodied in the childlike character of Father Quixote.

Father Quixote's obscenity marks the turning point in the novel. When the bishop arrives to question and censure him for his scandalous actions, the saintly and innocent priest defies his bureaucratic and pharisaical inquistor. Accused of keeping company with prostitutes, of associating with a communist, of drinking, of attending an obscene movie, and of helping a robber to escape capture, Father Quixote ably and calmly defends his actions and the purity of his motives. He even points out to the bishop that Marx wrote "a most moving tribute to religion" when he spoke of "The most heavenly ec-

stasies of religious fervor." Convinced that the man
is mad, the bishop orders Father Quixote locked in
his room and prohibits him from saying mass and
hearing confessions.

With the help of Teresa, however, Father Quixote escapes from his imprisonment and drives off
with the mayor toward Galicia. There he discovers
a village of corrupt priests who live off the super-
stitions of the Mexicans who inhabit the town. When
he hears that the wealthy villagers bid for the honor
of carrying the Virgin in the procession on their feast
day, Father Quixote becomes enraged: "We are
going into battle, Sancho. I need my armor." He
dons his collar and even his *pechero* and confronts
the crowd with their blasphemy. Like his fictional
counterpart who attempts to rescue what he believes to be a real woman held captive in the procession, Father Quixote tries to free the Virgin from her
greedy captors and demands, "Put down Our Lady.
How dare you . . . clothe her like that in money? It
would be better to carry her through the streets
naked." Before long, he stirs up a near riot, leading
the mayor to observe, "That's the most serious crime
you've committed so far." They head to the monastery of Osera for sanctuary, and on the way Father
Quixote is seriously injured when the police shoot
at their car.

Father Quixote's name, the name of his traveling companion, his assistance of the robber, the
locking up his books (chivalric in their way, they
include the Gospels and the writings of Saint John
of the Cross, Saint Teresa of Avila, and Saint Francis
de Sales), and his attack on the procession parallel
Cervantes's story and establish the romantic saintliness of Greene's simple-hearted hero. But he is a
very human saint, riddled by doubts. He wants to
believe "that it is all true" and "that want," he says,

"is the only certain thing I feel." Sharing the adventures of his mind, his acts of faith, chivalry, and simple kindness, the mayor is drawn deeply into the truth of this priest's fictional reality.

The two outcasts spend hours debating the philosophy of Karl Marx and Christianity during their journey, and Father Quixote daydreams of "how their journey would go on and on—the dream of deepening friendship and a profounder understanding, of a reconciliation even between their disparate faiths." And, indeed, this dream comes nearly true by the novel's end. The mayor suspects that in seeking Father Quixote's company he is searching for his lost innocence, "that youth when I half believed in your religion." Father Quixote reassures him that he has a "complete belief" in the prophet Marx, but the mayor remembers his old professor raising the question of doubt: "Without this uncertainty how could we live?" Father Quixote acknowledges the importance of doubt to the vitality of one's faith: "Oh, Sancho, Sancho, it's an awful thing not to have doubts." Father Quixote experiences the deadly effect of certitude on faith in a dream he has that Christ had been saved from the Cross by a legion of angels, whereupon the disciples cluster happily around and Mary smiles through her tears of joy: "There was no ambiguity, no room for doubt and no room for faith at all. The whole world knew with certainty that Christ was the son of God." He awakens with a prayer, "God save me from such a belief," and seeing the mayor still asleep, adds, "Save him too from belief."

These discourses on faith and doubt, Marx and Christ, finally lead to a central theme in the novel—that is, the inability to distinguish between fact and fiction, an inability that forces one to choose, to leap, in an act of faith, to a conclusion. The very fact that

Father Quixote claims to be descended from a fictional character raises the question as to what is true and what is fiction. Despite the protestations of his enemies that he is mad, Father Quixote blithely assumes the traits of his fictional namesake. As he explains to the mayor, "I am Father Quixote, and not Don Quixote. I tell you, I exist. My adventures are my own adventures, not his. . . . I have free will. I am not tethered to an ancestor who has been dead these four hundred years." And yet, of course, the parallels between the two men are clearly there. Greene allows the overlay of Cervantes's hero on his own to make the point that fiction and truth are inseparable. Early in the novel the Bishop of Motopo tells Father Quixote that "Perhaps we are all fictions, father, in the mind of God," and that it was only by tilting at windmills that Don Quixote found truth on his deathbed.

At the end of the novel, Father Leopoldo, a Trappist monk of the Osera monastery where Father Quixote has found refuge, reiterates the titular bishop's observation. Father Leopoldo was led to his faith through his reading the works of Descartes. He wanted to question everything in his search for an absolute truth and in the end, like Descartes, he accepted what appeared to be the nearest thing to truth: "But it was then that he had taken a greater leap than Descartes—a leap into the silent world of Osera." And so, Father Leopoldo observes, "Fact or fiction—in the end you can't distinguish between them—you just have to choose." When a skeptical American professor staying at the monastery questions Father Quixote's descent from a fictional character, Father Leopoldo replies, "Fact and fiction again, professor. So difficult to distinguish."

The final scene in the novel poignantly fuses the theme of the inseparability of illusion and reality

with that of the central importance of love and
truth—mad though their expression seems—as the
liberating forces of man's spirit in a world of narrow
conventions and dull sanity. In his final delirium
Father Quixote, who has been forbidden to say
mass, acts out a dream mass. He sleepwalks to the
altar and begins to intone the sacred ceremony,
while Father Leopoldo and the mayor watch in
wonder. He raises his empty hands and consecrates
the nonexistent bread, then the nonexistent wine.
Finally, appearing conscious that he is not alone in
the church, he takes the nonexistent Host between
his fingers and addresses Sancho: "*Compañero*,' he
said, 'you must kneel, *compañero*.' . . . The mayor
opened his mouth and felt the fingers, like a Host,
on his tongue." After administering the invisible
Host, Father Quixote dies. And when the mayor asks
if he actually received Communion, Father Leopoldo says, "You certainly did—in *his* mind."

The final fiction in this pantomimic mass carries
with it the themes of love and sacrifice, along with
doubt and faith. The mayor's life has been changed.
Frightened by mystery, he prefers to think there was
no Host: "I prefer Marx to mystery." An yet, he has
lost his freedom on the road from El Toboso because
he has experienced a revelation of doubt, and "to
doubt, he thought, is to lose the freedom of action."
He cannot be sure that he did not receive the Host,
and if he did, then he is no longer free to disbelieve
in the God of Father Quixote. Both the priest and
the Marxist transcend the literalness of their re-
spective faiths and are joined together in charity.
The rich ambiguity of faith has been planted like a
seed in the mayor's mind, a faith nourished by love,
for we are told that the love "which he had begun
to feel for Father Quixote seemed now to live and
grow in spite of the final separation and the final

silence." The foolish madman, the childlike innocent, descended from a fictional character, thus
leaves the mayor wondering "for how long . . . was
it possible for that love of his to continue? And to
what end?"

Looking through this novel back to Greene's
earlier works, one discovers the resurrection and
transformation of some of his major concerns. The
search for peace and innocence that compelled such
tormented characters as Scobie, Querry, and Castle
comes to rest in the character of Father Quixote,
who has found the city that Castle called Peace of
Mind. The intense debates between the atheist lieutenant and the whisky priest, between the communist Magiot and the ex-Catholic Brown, and between the radical Father Rivas and Doctor Plarr are
recapitulated and resolved by the understanding
that arises between the mayor and Father Quixote.
The threatening atmosphere of Mexico, Vietnam,
and Haiti finds new expression in the church of El
Toboso and the Guardia Civil of Spain that attempt
to capture and silence Father Quixote. Unlike
Greene's most famous hunted hero, the whisky
priest, Father Quixote travels with a great peace of
mind, leaving his fate in the hands of God—and,
ironically, his hunter, unlike the God-hating lieutenant in *The Power and the Glory*, is a representative of the Catholic church. The uncertainty of
God's existence that haunted such heroes as Maurice Bendrix and Querry is here transformed into a
vital and necessary condition for belief. The quest
for certainty, as Father Quixote points out, would
end only in the destruction of faith. Finally, the
theme of the inseparability of fact and fiction not
only represents Greene's comment on the importance of faith and free will but also suggests that his

own fiction—as well as that of Father Quixote—
goes beyond entertainment to embody the truth of
the human predicament. "Fact or fiction," as Father
Leopoldo reminds us, "in the end you can't distinguish between them."

3

Entertainments

Between 1932 and 1958 Greene published seven works that he labeled "entertainments": *Stamboul Train, A Gun for Sale, The Confidential Agent, The Ministry of Fear, The Third Man, Loser Takes All,* and *Our Man in Havana.* As pointed out earlier, Greene dissolved the divison between his entertainments and his novels in 1969 with the publication of *Travels with My Aunt,* but his labels had a clear purpose up to that point. They forewarned the reader, especially the critic and reviewer, what to expect. As Greene explained in a radio interview in 1955, in an entertainment "one is primarily interested in having an exciting story as in a physical action, with just enough character to give interest to the action." In the novel, on the other hand, "one is primarily interested in the character and the action takes a minor part."[1] He later characterized the difference between the two categories in terms of his manic and depressive periods: "The strain of writing a novel, which keeps the author confined for a period of years with his depressive self, is extreme and I have always sought relief in 'entertainments'—for melodrama as much as farce is an expression of a manic mood." With the publication of *The Comedians* in 1966 Greene began to see tragedy and comedy, the depressive and the manic, as

compatible with each other, and this insight, cou-
pled with his sense of the healing nature of love,
provided the wholeness of vision that developed in
his later works and that made the divisions of his
fiction into two types no longer necessary.

Kenneth Allott and Miriam Farris provide a useful distinction between Greene's novels and entertainments:

In general the entertainment has to be distinguished from
the novel by the comparative lack of development in the
characters, by the willful use of interesting background
for its own sake, and, more particularly perhaps, by the
freedom Greene allows himself in linking up the various
sections of his narrative by coincidences and improba-
bilities. After *Stamboul Train* the pattern of the entertainments may be as subtle as that of the novels, but it is
more easily achieved.[2]

With the exception of *Loser Takes All* and *Our Man
in Havana*, all of Greene's entertainments could appropriately be called thrillers, a popular form of fiction stemming from the nineteenth-century novel
and drama and characterized by melodramatic action. Murder, pursuit, hairbreadth escapes, dangerous intrigue, and happy endings are the lifeblood
of such works. What sets Greene's entertainments
apart from the contemporary thrillers is that through
this genre he manages to evoke a unique and compelling vision of the world. He weaves into the action and atmosphere of the thriller fascinatingly obsessive characters who, though not as fully drawn
as those in his novels, nevertheless embody a haunting sense of evil and depravity. Greene' first five
entertainments go beyond mere amusement by their
creation of a nightmarish image of life that is at once
terrifying and seductive.

In *Stamboul Train* Greene employs the closed
setting of the Orient Express to bring together a het-

erogeneous group of people. Carleton Myatt, a Jew-
ish currant merchant (drawn after T. S. Eliot's Mr.
Eugenides, the Smyrna merchant "with a pocket
full of currants"), is on his way to Constantinople to
conclude a business deal. Coral Musker, a chorus
girl with a bit part awaiting her in that city, loses
her virginity to Myatt out of gratitude for his sympathy for her. When she faints in the cold corridor
of the train, he gives up his first-class sleeper to her.
Paul Czinner, a political revolutionary, is returning
to Belgrade to lead a communist uprising that, he
discovers en route, started prematurely and, lacking
his leadership, was summarily put down by government forces. Mabel Warren, an alcoholic lesbian
journalist, boards the train at Cologne because she
recognizes Czinner and hopes to get an exclusive
story for her newspaper. Mabel is accompanied by
her girlfriend, Janet Pardoe, a beautiful but vain and
stupid girl, who is contrasted with the warmth and
cheerful pluck of Coral. (Greene later resurrected
the name Coral for the heroic and innocent Coral
Fellows in *The Power and the Glory*). Quin Savory,
a popular cockney novelist (Greene's hateful image
of what he himself might become), and Josef Grünlich, a thief eluding the police in Vienna, round out
the major figures on the train who, as David Pryce-
Jones has pointed out, "are being borne to a destiny
as much as to a destination."[3]

The story is divided into five parts, each one
corresponding to the major stops on the train line.
Most of the action, however, is confined to Subotica,
near the Hungarian border. There Czinner is arrested by the authorities, and Coral, because he
thrust some papers into her hand to mail for him, is
taken for his accomplice. Later Grünlich is locked
up with them after the police discover his gun in a
customs check. Myatt gets off the train at the next

stop and hires a car to take him back to Subotica where he hopes to find Coral.

Czinner meantime has been condemned to die for his treachery, Grünlich is sentenced to a month's imprisonment, and Coral to a day's confinement before she is repatriated. All three, however, manage to escape from the locked station where they are held captive, but during their flight Czinner is shot by the police. Coral returns to help him while Grünlich runs ahead and discovers Myatt, who has just arrived. He tells Myatt that he is alone and that they must drive on to avoid the military police, thus saving his life and leaving Czinner to die and Coral to fend for herself.

Coral knows she is foolish for loving Myatt and for expecting him to rescue her (though she does not realize that he made the attempt). "I'm tired of being decent, of doing the right thing," she exclaims, and wonders if Czinner, who is dying as they both hide in a shed from the police, is not in a similar position: "he had been faithful to people who could have been better served by cunning." Mabel Warren, meanwhile, on the trail of Czinner, turns up and carries Coral away to Vienna as her new lover.

Shortly after he arrives in Constantinople, Myatt plans to marry Janet Pardoe when he discovers that she is the niece of a businessman he must please in order to acquire a monopoly in the currant market. Greene's wandering Jew thus acknowledges, "It's about time I settled down," secure in the knowledge that his marriage "would have arranged far more than his domestic future; he would have bought Mr. Stein's business at Mr. Stein's figure, and Mr. Stein would have a nephew on the board and be satisfied."

Despite the happy ending for Myatt and Janet, the main theme of this story is the devastation that

is wrought by one's sense of failure or by the absence of love. Czinner is an innocent whose social
idealism proves inadequate to cope with the brutal
reality of politics, and he becomes tormented with
a sense of failure and guilt. His parents had starved
themselves that he might become a doctor, but he
later discovered the uselessness of his profession for
"his own people," the poor, because they could not
afford the treatments he prescribed for them. He is
haunted by multiple failures—as a son, as a doctor,
as a believer, and now, most painfully, as the leader
of an abortive revolution. After he is condemned to
die the "Sad and beautiful faces, thin from bad food,
old before their time, resigned to despair," pass before his mind. "They were the people he had
known, whom he attended and failed to save."

The critic John Atkins interestingly suggests
that Greene's obsession with failure here is related
to his disgust with sex.[4] Love, not to mention cheerful sexuality, is singularly absent from this novel-
istic version of Eliot's wasteland. Myatt substitutes
money and the big business deal for sexual satisfaction. His brief relationship with Coral is both
shallow and self-indulgent. "I hurt you," he half
apologizes to her. "It wasn't a picnic," she replies.
Their sexual encounter is not only antiromantic, it
is almost trivial. "A girl was expected to repay, that
was the point of all advice," Greene says (with an
interesting monetary metaphor) of her dutiful aban-
donment of her virginity. Within a couple of days
Myatt forgets Coral and is deep into the more satisfying body of big business. With Janet Pardoe he
acquires both a sexual and a corporate partnership.

The most repulsive character in the book is
Mabel Warren. A self-indulgent, sentimental drunk-
ard, she is filled with hatred for men and focuses
her venom on the fragile innocence of Czinner: "I'll

get him somehow. God damn his soul." She, too, is a failure, a lesbian whose love is sterile and self-condemning. She is faced always with the fact "that she gave no enjoyment and gained herself no more than an embittered sense of insufficiency." Greene rewards her at the end of the story by allowing her Myatt's cast-off mistress. Mabel turns Coral into an "exclusive"—"a dream . . . of Coral in pyjamas pouring out coffee, Coral in pyjamas mixing a cocktail, Coral asleep in the redecorated and rejuvenated flat." This for Greene's innocent dancer who only days earlier fantasized a beautiful wedding party with Myatt. "It's too good to be true," Coral remarks after her night of love with Myatt. Her prospects with Mabel affirm the death of fruitful sexuality and love that are, indeed, too good to be true in the sterile and soulless world of this story.

One of the most fascinating characters in the book is Josef Grünlich. Totally selfish and brutal, he is the male counterpart of Mabel Warren, only he exhibits his sexual perversion through violence. Like Mabel, he is physically ugly, a fat man "who ran his hands between his pants and trousers and adjusted the revolver which hung between his legs by a piece of string twisted around a button." The image of the gun as phallus reveals the punishing nature of Grünlich's sexuality. Under the pretense of seducing the wealthy Herr Kolber's maid, Anna, he steals her employer's money. Greene's description of these two "lovers" is grotesque. Anna has uneven, discolored teeth and displays "a horrible middle-aged coquetry" as she holds a towel before her legs to hide them from Grünlich's view. Grünlich talks to her in baby language, a sickening parody of innocent romantic love: "What had the pretty Anna got now then? A great big man? Oh, how he will rumple you." But sex is not what he is after,

and he does not rumple her; rather, he goes to the
next room to get the money from the safe. Herr Kolber returns, and Grünlich shoots and kills him.

His first murder invigorates his pride, and he
imagines people marveling at him: "There's Josef.
He killed Kolber at Vienna, but they never caught
him. He's never been caught." In the last chapter
Myatt sees Grünlich in a Turkish restaurant. The fat
man simply waves at him and grins. Among Czinner's last thoughts before he dies is "how hard it
would be for a Christian to reconcile the escape [of
Grünlich] with his own death."

The "happy ending" of *Stamboul Train*—the
coupling of Myatt and Janet, Coral and Mabel, along
with Grünlich's escape—is an appropriate com-
mentary on the nature of justice in a world where
love and innocence have no place. And because this
world that Greene has created offers no hope, there
can be no redemption. Financial deals, lesbian fantasies, and a murder with impunity are the parodic
life signs of this wasteland; love is traded for money,
sex for violence, and innocence for death or despair.

A Gun for Sale extends the hopeless image of
the world found in *Stamboul Train* but focuses it
through the character of its hero, James Raven.
"Murder didn't mean much to Raven," the story
opens. "It was just a new job." Raven is a bitter,
solitary, and desperate young man. His looks dis-
figured by a harelip, he is despised by women and
expresses his sexuality and hostility, like Grünlich,
through his revolver. He also resembles Pinkie
Brown, for he is an outcast who is driven by an "in-
grown virginity" and a hatred for a capitalistic world
that has betrayed his childhood innocence. When
he was a boy, his father was hanged in prison, after
which his mother slit her throat. Raven walked into

the kitchen and saw "her head nearly off—she'd
sawn at it with—a bread knife," and these grotesque
memories haunt the rest of his days. Unlike Dickens's sentimental treatment of his orphans (their
good natures survive the beatings), Greene depicts
his hero as one whose corrupted childhood dooms
him to a life of violence and distrust. As Raven says,
the ugly have no chance: "They [the parents] have
a good time and what do they mind if someone's
born ugly? Three minutes in bed or against the wall,
and then a lifetime for the one that's born."

The theme of *A Gun for Sale* is betrayal. A mil-
lionaire armament maker named Sir Marcus, in
order to increase his profits, attempts to establish a
war scare by having his associate, Davis, hire Raven
to murder the minister for war. After Raven kills the
minister, Davis double-crosses him by paying him
with stolen bank notes, with numbers known to the
police. When Raven discovers the betrayal, he sets
out to find Davis and obtain revenge. Meanwhile,
James Mather, a detective engaged to marry Anne
Crowder, follows the trail that Raven leaves with
his marked bills, not realizing that Raven is the same
person who murdered the government official.

After Raven and Anne are improbably thrown
together, he tells her the half-truth that Davis killed
the minister for war. Believing that there will not
be a war if he kills Davis, Anne agrees to join Raven
in his pursuit. Like Coral Musker, Anne is a chorus
girl—a seedy innocent—who unintentionally becomes involved in dangerous intrigue. She pities
Raven and gradually wins his confidence. Having
been recently betrayed to the police by a member
of "his own class," a crooked doctor whom he went
to for surgery to disguise his harelip, Raven is un-
derstandably slow to accept Anne's intimacy. "You
can trust me all right" she tells him, and his need

to confess—a characteristic need among Greene's solitary heroes—leads him to reveal the details of his past, from his betrayal by the chaplain at the orphanage through that of the doctor and Davis: "His happiness was incomplete till she knew everything, till he had shown his trust completely."

But Anne, despite her sincerity at the moment, is not bound by the seal of the confessional. Raven's admission to the murder of the minister for war, combined with his subsequent shooting of an innocent policeman, leads Anne to betray him. She tells Mather the whole story. Meanwhile Raven traces Davis to Midland Steel and the office of Sir Marcus. Davis informs Raven that Anne has betrayed him: "She wasn't a friend of yours. Why are the police here if she didn't—who else could have known—?" In killing Davis, Raven attempts to destroy the entire mad world that has tormented him since childhood: "he plugged two bullets in where one would do, as if he were shooting the whole world in the person of stout, moaning, bleeding Mr. Davis. And so he was. For a man's world is his life, and he was shooting that." His final message is that "There was no one outside your own brain whom you could trust; not a doctor, not a priest, not a woman."

There is a sense in this and other Greene stories that one is predestined to destruction. From the beginning, the whisky priest in *The Power and the Glory* consciously moved to his betrayal at the hands of the mestizo. And here Raven is a victim of social forces that destine him to this ultimate betrayal. Earlier, when he saw a crêche in the window of a Nottwich shop, Raven stared at the swaddled child and thought, "'the little bastard'—because he was educated and knew what the child was in for: *the damned Jews* and the double-crossing Judas."

Like Christ, "he had been marked from his birth for this end, to be betrayed in turn by everyone until every avenue into life was safely closed. . . . How could he have expected to escape the commonest betrayal of all, to go soft on a skirt?" As he leaves Midland Steel, Raven is shot in the back by Mather's assistant. Death comes to him in the form of unbearable pain. Like Pinkie Brown's, his tormented soul is finally released into oblivion: "It was as if he had to deliver this pain as a woman delivers a child. . . . At last it came out of him, and he followed his only child into a vast desolation."

The story properly ends here, with Raven's death, but Greene adds a final chapter to comment on the bleak world that continues to deteriorate. The war that Anne hoped to avert still haunts the scene ("Men were fighting beasts," she thinks, "they needed war"), and her future with Mather, their happy marriage, is momentarily darkened by her sense of failure. "You don't understand," she tells Mather. "I *did* fail." But "she forgot it herself completely when the train drew into London." Mather receives a promotion, and Anne, with her memory of failure happily exchanged for the prospects of marriage upon her arrival home, looks toward a bright future. Presumably, she overcomes her realization that in Raven's dead mind "she was preserved forever with the chaplain who had tried to frame him, with the doctor who had telephoned to the police." As the train pulls into the station, she exclaims, "with a sigh of unshadowed happiness, 'we're home.'" And so, Greene rescues his Judas figure from guilt and self-recrimination and rewards her with the promise of a happy marriage, a fitting tribute to Raven's sense of outrage at the injustice of his blighted world.

Underlying the theme of betrayal in this work is Greene's despair of true love and his depiction of its perversions. The Christmas setting for the story ironically underscores the absence of Christian charity in the cold, bleak city of Nottwich, where most of the action takes place. The world is huddled not only against the cold but against the fear of war. And, as Raven says, "There's always been a war for me." He has never known love or even human warmth. His only affection is for a kitten. When he does open himself to another person and shares his thoughts and feelings, he pays the price for that intimacy with his death. Sir Marcus, like Krogh, exhibits no human feelings and lives only to increase his wealth and power. Davis can only enjoy the company of seedy girls who satisfy his lust and share his sensuality. Mather is too much of an organization man to care deeply about love: "I always want to be on the side that organizes." He seeks security, not love: "He liked to be certain, to feel that one day quite inevitably he would marry Anne Crowder."

The only two characters who share a bond of strong mutual love are Acky, a deranged defrocked clergyman and Tiny, his evil old wife. These two ugly, brutal characters run the bawdy house in which Davis tries to kill Anne. Greene seems to delight in the irony that love and fidelity, which are lacking among the other characters, take deep root in this grotesque couple. Obsessed with his removal from the church for some sexual offense, Acky screams obscenities at Raven and quotes Saint Paul. Acting as proprietors of lust and filled with hatred for intruders into their bizarre sanctuary, Acky and Tiny nevertheless enjoy a long and happy marriage. In the final chapter of the story Acky is writing still another letter to his bishop to convince him of the injustice done him, arguing that "A little carnality may be forgiven even to a man of my cloth." Proud of her husband's lyrical defense, Tiny reassures him of her fidelity: "I won't ever leave you. I won't leave you, not even when I'm dead. Never, never, never. . . ." Greene's final picture of this unwholesome domesticity asserts the irony that love and fidelity are the spoils of the mad predators of lust: "the two old vicious faces regarded each other with the complete belief, the awe and mutual suffering of a great love, while they affirmed their eternal union." And so love goes, in Greeneland.

Raven's statement that "There's always been a war for me" is echoed in Greene's description of D., the anonymous hero of his next entertainment, *The Confidential Agent*: "He carried the war with him. Wherever D. was, there was a war." A university lecturer, D. abandons academe to carry out a secret mission in England. His unnamed republic is in the midst of a civil war, and D. has been sent to negotiate a contract with the British mine owners for badly needed coal. Despite his education and middle-class origins, D. is forced by the treacherous times into the role of a hunted outcast, like Raven and the whisky priest. He knows that even if his side wins the war, the have-nots with whom he has sided will not trust him because he is a bourgeois. "We just have to choose our side," he asserts, "and neither side will trust us, of course." In a godless world of violence and suffering, his commitment to a cause at least gives a purpose to his life, a purpose no longer served by the lecture halls. Driven by his pity and compassion for the suffering of the poor and innocent of his country, D. resembles Czinner in his relentless struggle to bring about social justice, and, like Czinner, he fails in his mission. He does not acquire the coal but manages, however, with the help of some teddy boys, to dynamite the pithead, thus making it impossible for his enemies to get the coal as well.

Although narrated in the third person, the story focuses the action through the consciousness of D., first as the hunted and then as the hunter. In the first part of the book D. is pursued by enemy agents and the English police, and he is spied on by his own distrustful contacts. The turning point in the hunt comes with the murder of an innocent child named Else, whose only crime was a brief association with D. Her murder symbolizes for him all of the brutality and injustice he is fighting against, and it transforms him into a savage hunter obsessed with revenge. Like Raven, who attempts to shoot the whole mad world by shooting Davis, D. focuses his rage on K. "I've had a gang of traitors after me ever since I came across. Now I'm going to do the shooting," he exclaims. "Rage was like vitality in his veins," and he swears that "from now on he would be the hunter, the watcher, the marksman in the mews."

The cocked gun and explosive rage of Greene's hero, however, are given a comic conclusion. D. pursues Else's killer, one of D.'s fellow agents named K., and shoots at him, but the bullet misses its mark and K. dies moments later of fright. Too much the university scholar, D. "would never make an executioner." Greene's sense of humor at this point in a tense story gives the conventional scheme of the thriller a new twist and salvages the essential humanity of its hero, a man whose instincts have been shaped by the classics of romance to which he has dedicated his professional life. On the other hand, D.'s blasé and joking attitude about K.'s death—"I should like to be charged with an honest malice-

aforethought murder for a change," he says to
Rose—trivializes his earlier outrage at the murdered innocence of Else and violates his character
as avenger.

Like so many of Greene's heroes, D. falls in love
with a girl young enough to be his daughter. In this
instance the girl is Rose Cullen, the daughter of the
mine owner to whom D.'s mission is directed. Contrasted with Anne Crowder, who betrays Raven,
Rose serves as a loyal guardian angel who sees D.
through a tangle of intrigue, betrayals, and murders
to final escape. In this respect, she resembles her
namesake in *Brighton Rock*.

Like Raven and Pinkie, D. cannot enjoy normal
sexuality. He feels an immense tenderness for Rose,
not only "because she might have been his daughter" but also because "She made no demands on
him for passionate love." D.'s passion died with his
wife, who was shot by mistake in the civil war, and
Greene forces the association of sexuality with
death in this story. After the death of K., D. takes
Rose into his arms, and "everything was there except desire." "It was as if he had made himself a
eunuch for his people's sake," Greene notes. The
act of desire was an act of faith, D. reasons, and he
had lost his faith in the world. And so Greene allows
only a paternal tenderness to grow out of this wasteland; sexual fulfillment, like innocence, belongs to
the dead.

The story ends with D.'s reunion with Rose
aboard a ship that is returning to his country. Aware
of D.'s fidelity to his dead wife, Rose says, "When
you are dead, she can have you. I can't compete
then, and we'll be dead a long, long time." But as
the ship moves into the dark toward D.'s warworn
home, Rose concludes the story with the plea,

"You'll be dead very soon: you needn't tell me that, but now . . ."

War, one assumes, will ultimately destroy their hopes for a bright future based on love and justice, and so Rose and D. must accept their "happy ending" in the fragile present moment. The pathos of Rose's plea echoes Matthew Arnold's desperate cry in "Dover Beach":

> Ah, love, let us be true
> To one another! for the world, which seems
> To lie before us like a land of dreams,
> So various, so beautiful, so new,
> Hath really neither joy, nor love, nor light,
> Nor certitude, nor peace, nor help for pain . . .

For these early entertainments, Greene has appropriated Arnold's nightmarish vision of a world "where ignorant armies clash by night." But he at least grants his impotent hero and Rose a mutual trust in each other as they huddle against the cold of a crumbling civilization where, Greene notes, "There was no trust anywhere."

Although *A Gun for Sale* and *The Confidential Agent* evoke an atmosphere of anxiety and violence created by the rumors and vague threats of war, Greene's next work, *The Ministry of Fear* (1943), reflects the actual trauma of London during the height of the German blitz. Despite his use of factual, contemporary setting, however, Greene ironically renders the atmosphere of this story in terms that suggest an extended nightmare, one from which his tormented hero, Arthur Rowe, only partially recovers.

The main theme of this book is the isolating and destructive force of pity, a theme that looks toward *The Heart of the Matter*. Arthur Rowe has poisoned his wife because he could not bear to watch her

suffer from an incurable disease. Although the court
found him innocent of any crime, he nurses a powerful sense of guilt for his actions and continues to
be driven by a disproportionate sense of responsibility for the suffering of those around him. As
Greene observes of his hero, "People could always
get things out of him by wanting them enough; it
broke his precarious calm to feel that people suffered. Then he would do anything for them. Anything."

The above description would accurately apply
to Scobie as well as to Rowe, but unlike Scobie,
Rowe has analyzed his compulsive sense of pity and
traces its origin to his loss of childhood innocence.
The story thus opens with Rowe entering a local fair,
which "called him like innocence: it was entangled
in childhood, with vicarage gardens and girls in
white summer frocks and the smell of herbaceous
borders and security." The appeal of the fair is especially strong for him because of the war that is
raging, with its daily reminders of the corrupt adult
world filled with suffering, betrayal, and death.

Ironically, Rowe's attendance at the fair leads
to his becoming a hunted man. He wins a cake that,
unknown to him, contains a microfilm of secret
naval plans placed there by a spy ring. After he returns to his room, a malignant cripple named Poole,
one of the Nazi agents who constitute the Ministry
of Fear, visits Rowe in an attempt to kill him and
retrieve the film. Poole puts hyoscine in Rowe's tea,
the same poison that Rowe used to kill his wife. Too
hot to swallow, the tea's "odd flavour haunted him
like something remembered. . . . Life struck back at
him like a scorpion, over the shoulder." Only seconds later a German bomb explodes, destroying his
flat, and Rowe is soundly returned to the terrors and
chaos of the actual world. The fact that someone

wants to kill him for no apparent reason twists his
sense of reality into a Kafkaesque nightmare.

He later attends a séance at the home of Mrs.
Bellairs, the same woman who told his fortune at
the fair. As in T. S. Eliot's "Wasteland," superstition
has replaced traditional Christian belief. During the
course of the "unholy rites of Mrs. Bellairs," a spirit
voice begins to pose a question: "Arthur, why did
you kill . . ." and seconds later a member of the
group is apparently stabbed to death with Rowe's
knife. Rowe thought: "Somebody here *has* killed
him—it was fantastic, more fantastic really than that
he should have done it himself." Willi Hilfe, a
young Austrian relief worker (who pretends to be
Rowe's friend but who actually masterminds the
Nazi spy ring) advises Rowe to go underground.

The murder at the séance turns out to be a con-
trivance to drive Rowe into hiding. Thinking he is
wanted by the police for a murder he did not commit, haunted by the actual murder of his wife, and
aware of the fact that someone wants him killed,
Rowe has a dream about his lost childhood—"Tea
on the lawn, evensong, croquet, the old ladies calling"—and declares, "This isn't real life anymore."
He becomes filled with horror at the thought of what
a child becomes, "and what the dead must feel
watching the change from innocence to guilt and
powerless to stop it." His dream then shifts to focus
on his inordinate sense of pity when, as a child, he
witnessed a dog tormenting a rat, and, unable to
bear the sight of the rat's pain any longer, he crushed
its head with a cricket bat. Neither his nurse nor his
mother realized that what had come over him was
"the horrible and horrifying emotion of pity," the
sentiment that later would bring him to kill his wife
and isolate him from the rest of the world.

In the next chapter, appropriately entitled "Out of Touch," Rowe loses his capability to fantasize and to dream: "He wanted to dream, but all he could practice now was despair." Homeless and sick with the realization of the selfishness in his "mercy killing," he finds support and comfort in Willi's sister, Anna. The powerful "They" of the Ministry of Fear arrange to bring the two together in order to kill them. "They want us both," Rowe suddenly realizes, and when he opens the lid of a suitcase that is supposed to contain books, a bomb goes off. Anna is spared, but Rowe is seriously injured.

In Book Two, entitled "The Happy Man," Rowe is a victim of amnesia from the bomb blast and is a patient in Dr. Forester's nursing home in the country. His identity card says that his name is Richard Digby, but Rowe remembers nothing of his past. Through violence he is ironically returned to a sort of childlike innocence. His amnesia allows him to enjoy an Arcadian existence for a time, and, surrounded by sunlight, trees, and gentle attendants, he is unaware of the war raging in London, of his murder trial, and of his hunted past: "Now, with no memories nearer than his boyhood, he was entirely free." And thus, for the moment, ignorance is indeed bliss.

The reader soon realizes that Dr. Forester is a member of the network of spies whose job it is to keep Rowe out of action. After Rowe discovers a pathetic old man named Stone, whom Dr. Forester keeps in a straitjacket, he feels "capable of murder for the release of that tormented creature," and confronts Dr. Forester with his cruelty. The doctor retaliates by telling Rowe his real name and showing him a newspaper photograph. He hopes that by letting him know that he is a murderer he will cause Rowe to commit suicide or go insane. Rowe's response to this sudden and brutal disclosure is described with the same metaphor of childbirth that Greene used in depicting Raven's death: "his head was racked with pain as other memories struggled to get out like a child out of its mother's body" and "his brain reeled with the horror of returning life." Thus begins Rowe's rebirth and return to the complex, sordid world from which he enjoyed only a temporary reprieve.

The next two sections, "Bits and Pieces" and "The Whole Man," chart the process of Rowe's gradual integration as he acquires complete self-knowledge. He expresses anew his disillusionment with life: "I thought life was much simpler and—grander." Mr. Prentice of Scotland Yard, who is investigating the spy ring operation, helps Rowe to sort out some of the bits and pieces of his past as the action continues at a rapid pace. In the course of a drive together, Prentice articulates the theme of pity when he says that "Pity is a terrible thing. People talk about the passion of love. Pity is the worst passion of all: we don't outlive it like sex." Ironically, Rowe fails to grasp the significance of Prentice's remarks. Still unsure of his past, he surmises "that I led a dull humdrum life."

Meanwhile the number of murders and deaths continues to multiply, including Dr. Forester's chloroforming of his patient, Stone, after which Johns (Dr. Forester's admiring and idealistic assistant) murders Dr. Forester to save him from the "interminable proceedings of the law courts." As the spy network collapses, the last chapter focuses on the triangle of Anna, Willi, and Rowe. Anna's love for Rowe leads her to shield him from his past. Like the spies, she does not want his memory to return, but her motive is Rowe's continued happiness. Of course, in Greene's world adults cannot enjoy their innocence for any length of time, and despite Anna's intervention, Rowe regains his blighted past.

Discovering that Willi is the leader of the spy ring, Rowe attempts to obtain from him the film of the naval secrets. After being disarmed, Willi offers Rowe a bargain: the film and the missing piece of Rowe's past (the killing of his wife) for his escape. Rowe refuses to bargain, obtains the film, but Willi proposes a final deal: he will complete Rowe's memory in exchange for a revolver and a single bullet with which to commit suicide. Rowe again refuses, but Willi insists on revealing the details of Rowe's trial for the murder of his wife anyway. His curiosity satiated, Rowe feels himself a whole man once again, and in still another act of pity, allows Willi to commit suicide with his revolver.

The whole man, then, is the man steeped in suffering, who faces the terror of life with an isolating pity and a wistful longing for lost innocence. The "happy" ending of the story finds Rowe and Anna sitting together in silence: "they were on the edge of their ordeal." They "must watch each other like enemies because they loved each other so much." Fear, distrust, and guilt now haunt their love. The Ministry of Fear has done its work and has gone well beyond the limited aims of winning a war or changing a constitution. As Rowe puts it, "It was a Ministry as large as life to which all who loved belong."

Despite the implausible coincidences, the sometimes shaky fusion of spy narrative with somber reflections on innocence and pity, the surprise explosions that help set the melodramatic plot in motion, and the failure of Greene to present a rounded villain in the character of Willi Hilfe, *The Ministry of Fear* surpasses the earlier entertainments in its presentation of the terror of life, a vision deeply felt and compellingly rendered by Greene through the battered sensitivity and hopeless arrogance of his hero. The nightmarish atmosphere of war-torn London is the precise psychological equivalent of Rowe's devastated mind. The enemy lurks both without and within, in the German bombers and at the dark corners of the human mind.

Furthermore, the book develops a number of ironies not found in Greene's earlier stories. Rowe's attraction to innocence, for example, makes him a victim of violence. His anguish over the suffering of others leads him to become a sinister force of violence himself. To shield himself from suffering he kills his wife, wants to kill Stone, and allows Willi to kill himself. He is hunted by the Ministry of Fear because, we are told, he loved, but Rowe misleads us here. His selfishness and quiet arrogance are the forces that actually motivate his most important actions and shape his emotional commitments to others. And thus the victim of the Ministry of Fear is actually the victim of his own pity, "the worst passion of all."

Greene's next entertainment, *The Third Man*, was, in his words, "never written to be read but only to be seen." Alexander Korda asked him to write a film for Carol Reed and, finding it impossible to write a screenplay without first writing a story, he produced *The Third Man*. Greene is quite right to assert that the film is superior to the book because it is "the finished state of the story." The stark location scenes, the brilliant acting by Orson Welles (Harry Lime), Trevor Howard (Colonel Calloway), and Joseph Cotten (Rollo Martins), and the now famous zither theme music fleshed out the bare bones of Greene's brief story.

The plot is an intriguing one. Harry Lime of the International Relief Agency in Vienna offers his former schoolmate, Rollo Martins, a writer of westerns, the opportunity to describe the occupation of the city. When Rollo arrives, however, he discovers that Lime is dead. He suspects that his friend has been murdered and begins his own investigation into the circumstances of his death. He interviews Harry's friends; his mistress, Anna Schmidt; and his landlord. The landlord reveals that he saw three men carrying a body to the sidewalk after Harry was hit by a truck, but the police insist that only two men were involved. And so Rollo sets out to find the mysterious third man.

Rollo later learns that Harry is involved in a penicillin racket and that he has fabricated his death in order to elude capture by the police. And thus, ironically, Rollo's earlier search for the third man turns out to be a search for Harry himself. Once Rollo discovers that his friend has enriched himself at the expense of innocent children who died from the contaminated penicillin, his search for Lime leads him out of his schoolboy idealism to a realization of evil and to self-knowledge.

The Lime who was Rollo's hero for twenty years seems irreconcilable with Lime the racketeer. Every memory of Rollo's easy friendship and confidence is shattered by the revelation. He finally arranges a meeting with Lime on a huge Ferris wheel that lifts them high above the devastated city. Rollo is startled at the youthful appearance of his friend: "evil was like Peter Pan—it carried with it the horrifying and horrible gift of eternal youth." Like Pinkie and Pyle, Lime has never grown up, and his innocence is therefore that much more diabolical. He mocks his writer friend's meager income and announces, "I earn thirty thousand free. It's the fashion. In these days, old man, nobody thinks in terms of human beings." And, seen from the great height of the wheel, the people below do indeed seem less than human, and the imagery thus reinforces Lime's brutal arrogance.

Lime's last stand against the police takes place in the great sewer tunnels that run beneath the city, a sordid version of Allan Quatermain's voyage along the underground river to the city of Milosis. Leading the police, Rollo tracks Lime downstream and shoots him. Wounded and in pain, Lime collapses at the end of a passageway. Rollo finds him nearly dead and hears him utter the words "Bloody fool," a phrase meant either for himself ("some sort of act of contrition") or for Rollo. In any event, Rollo cannot bear the suffering of his fallen idol and puts a bullet through him.

In the last chapter Harry Lime has his second funeral, and Rollo Martins wins Harry's discarded mistress, Anna Schmidt. Colonel Calloway, the narrator, observes the couple and thinks: "it was like the end of a story except that before they turned out of sight her hand was through his arm—which is how a story usually begins."

Greene handles the theme of betrayal here in a new way. Usually his betrayed heroes are sympathetic characters, such as Raven and the whisky priest, but Greene portrays Lime as a monstrous villain. In the name of social justice and for the protection of the innocent he must be destroyed. Rollo's betrayal of his old friend thus anticipates the relationship between Fowler and Pyle in *The Quiet American*. In order to remain human and to save the innocent, Fowler turns Pyle over to the communists to be killed. But there is another dimension to these two betrayals: both Rollo and Fowler are in love with their adversaries' mistresses, Anna and

Phuong, and so they reap not only social justice but personal romantic rewards for their betrayals. Greene's heroes are motivated by personal concerns rather than abstract ones. The three particulars that drive Rollo are his schoolboy memories, his visit to the children's hospital where he sees the damage caused by Harry's greed, and his relationship with Anna. Harry, on the other hand, resembles Pyle in that he does not think in terms of human beings. Both men possess a form of parodic innocence. "You've never grown up," Rollo tells Lime; similarly, Fowler observes the youthful aspect of Pyle. Nevertheless, Lime's arrogance and greed, like Pyle's childlike idealism, lead to the wholesale suffering and death of those around him.

The structural pattern for this book derives from Conrad's *Heart of Darkness*. Green even names one of the minor characters Kurtz. Rollo's search for Lime parallels that of Marlow for Kurtz. Both Lime and Kurtz are mysterious, evil figures who dwell in the symbolic darkness (the unconscious) of the sewers and the jungle. For most of both works these villains are hidden away and only partially realized through secondhand reports about their characters and actions. Rollo's search, like Marlow's, gradually becomes a quest for personal meaning and self-knowledge. Lime and Kurtz represent the malignant alter egos of the incomplete idealistic heroes. Both Rollo and Marlow thus grow obsessed with the need to come face to face with these corrupted men (both of whom once held distinguished and responsible positions). And Lime and Kurtz both die uttering ambiguous judgments ("Bloody fool" and "The horror, the horror") that suggest their awareness of their corruption. Finally, both Rollo and Marlow, having confronted their unconscious selves, are changed men, aware of the power of darkness, which they now realize resides within themselves. When Calloway tells Rollo that he will overlook Rollo's mercy killing of Lime ("We'll forget that bit"), Rollo replies, "I never shall." And so, despite the happy ending with Rollo walking away arm in arm with Anna, Lime's death remains fixed in Rollo's consciousness like the fatal awareness of his loss of all his youthful dreams and happiness.

Like *The Third Man, Loser Takes All* was also written for the screen. Despite its cleverness and wit, it is a slight piece compared with the earlier entertainments. A middle-aged accountant named Bertram and his bride Cary are invited by his employer, Herbert Dreuther (called the Gom, for Grand Old Man), to be his guests at Monte Carlo during their honeymoon. But when the Gom fails to show up, Bertram has to devise a way to pay his hotel bills while awaiting his employer. He calls on his mathematical training to create a system at roulette and, using that method, wins five million francs. He spends this money to buy valuable stocks in his company from a stockholder who happens to be down on his luck at the roulette table. He intends to use these stocks in a scheme to get back at the Gom for failing to keep his promise. All of his financial manipulations, meanwhile, have lost him his bride, who says, "Darling, you've been very lucky and you've won a lot of money, but I don't like you anymore." She leaves him and takes up with a poor but romantic younger man.

Greene suggests that the devil is working on Bertram's behalf: "But the devil was certainly in my system and win I did." The Gom, on the other hand, is a God figure, reminiscent of Beckett's Godot. This deus ex machina finally arrives on his ship, *The Seagull* (recalling the sexually inspiring holy gull in *The*

Comedians), and discloses a plan whereby Bertram
can win back his bride. The plan consists simply of
his getting rid of all the wealth he has accumulated.
Meanwhile Cary's boyfriend has himself become
addicted to winning, so Bertram turns over his
money to him, announcing, "But it's loser takes all,"
and walks off with Cary. He also relinquishes his
deal with the stockholder. The Gom thus exorcises
the obsessive devil that nearly ruined a marriage
and rewards Bertram with a promotion to chief accountant. The reconciled couple looks toward a
bright, loving future together as Bertram tears into
pieces the great roulette system that temporarily
possessed him and blinded him to the importance
of love.

Unlike Krogh and Sir Marcus, the Gom is one
of Greene's few good capitalists. This may be due
in part to the fact that the Gom is drawn loosely after
Alexander Korda, Greene's respected friend. The
Gom controls most of the action of the story without
appearing in it. He invites Bertram and Cary to
spend their honeymoon in a place he knows they
cannot afford, and by failing to show up and bail
them out, he tests their love for each other. When
Bertram becomes corrupted by his system—and ar-
rogantly attempts to overthrow the Gom himself—
the Gom (with assumed omniscience) waits until
Bertram realizes that he cannot have both love and
wealth. He then intervenes and imparts the wisdom
necessary for Bertram to secure his bride. Ironically,
the capitalist Gom counsels him to relinquish his
wealth as the means of winning love. The benev-
olent industrialist, who has suffered four broken
marriages, has acquired his wisdom through bitter
experience and now, playing God, brings hope to
his naive employee.

In *The Third Man* and *Loser Takes All* Greene's interest lies in the plots more than in the characters. Bertram, Cary, and the Gom are all thinly drawn characters. Consequently, when Greene attempts to add thematic weight to these figures—as when he notes that Cary bore the sign of "Original Innocence" and "would always until old age look at the world with the eyes of a child"—they were unable to support it. Cary's innocence, for example, comes across as silly when she remarks after their hurried civil wedding ceremony, "I don't feel I've been married," but adds, "It's fun not being married." The theme of innocence is trivialized here, even as it is overdramatized in Rollo's Arcadian reflections in *The Third Man*. Although the characters are not large or complicated enough to embody Greene's serious themes, *Loser Takes All* demonstrates the author's ability to create a crisp, good-humored narrative, a talent fully realized in his next entertainment, *Our Man in Havana*.

Our Man in Havana is the last and best of Greene's entertainments. It surpasses the earlier works in depth of characterization and subtlety of theme and presents a comic vision of the world that anticipates *The Comedians* and *Monsignor Quixote*. The label "entertainment" for this book fails to disclose its real genre. Greene more accurately describes the work as "a fairy story" set "at some indeterminate date in the future."

The plot captures a comic view of life that Greene has denied his previous heroes and invests his new protagonist with the unique sanity of the clown. James Wormwold, a middle-aged Englishman who has been selling vacuum cleaners in Havana for fifteen years, has been left to care for his daughter Milly after his wife, whom he still loves, deserted him. When the story opens, he has been separated from his wife for five years, and the seventeen-year-old Milly continues to put a financial strain on him through her extravagance. His main purpose in life is to make her happy, but now he has nearly run out of money. When he is approached out of the blue by Hawthorne, an agent for the British secret service, who asks him to be MI5's "man in Havana," he reluctantly accepts the offer so that he can continue to finance Milly's education and girlish whims. At the same time, he is keenly aware of the absurdity of his role as a spy.

He quickly gets into the swing of things and invents a number of spies by borrowing names from the country club registry. He puts these fictional characters on his payroll and writes their reports to the home office in london. He even sends drawings of a fictional atomic installation based on sketches of one of his premium sales items, the Atomic Pile Cleaner. These elaborate reports win the praise and support of the officials in London, who are so pleased with his work that they send him a secretary, Beatrice, to help him expand his operation. Wormwold gradually falls in love with her while continuing to shower Milly with affection and favors.

The story reaches a climax when one of Wormwold's fictional characters, a young aviator named Raul, is actually killed by counterespionage forces. Wormworld is stunned, and asks, "Can we write human beings into existence?" The villain, a man named Carter, then attempts to poison Wormwold at a banquet, but forewarned by Dr. Hasselbacher, Wormwold's philosophic German friend, he gives his contaminated whisky to a dog sitting at his feet. As he later tells Beatrice, "I have come back victorious. The dog it was that died." The distinction between fiction and reality is further blurred when Carter murders Dr. Hasselbacher. At this point Wormwold confesses to Beatrice that his entire spy operation is a fiction and sets off to avenge his friend's murder. Wormwold, like D. in *The Confidential Agent*, is an inept marksman. He shoots Carter's Dunhill by mistake and his intended victim is outraged at the destruction of his expensive pipe. Nevertheless, he does finally shoot Carter, but, to maintain the comic tone, Greene simply reports this action later and does not describe it.

After Carter's death Wormwold is ordered to report to London and, to his embarrassment, he is awarded an Order of the British Empire. Besides the medal, the home office offers Wormwold an instructorship in the school of espionage. As the story ends, he and Beatrice plan their marriage, and Milly shows signs of accepting the fact that she will have to share her father's love with another woman. Beatrice's concern for the future, however, is that Wormwold "would never be quite mad enough" to continue to sustain them in a world that seems to run according to the logic of Alice's Wonderland.

Many of Greene's old subjects, themes, and characters reappear here. The subject of Catholicism, for example, is touched on lightly in Wormwold's promise to his wife to raise Milly a Catholic. Wormwold's hunt after the murderer, Carter, recalls Greene's previous hunters, though here he does not dwell on the chase. Captain Segura, Havana's chief of police, is reminiscent of the lieutenant in *The Power and the Glory*. The villain Carter resembles Davis in *A Gun for Sale*. Greene also resurrects the theme of innocence, as in Wormwold's plea, "Don't learn from experience, Milly. It ruins our peace and our lives."

Nevertheless, Greene weaves into the old fabric of this work a deeply felt relationship between Wormwold and his daughter. Milly gives shape to her father's life. He loves her, feels deeply responsible for her, and directs all of his energy toward ensuring her happiness. As Dr. Hasselbacher tells him, "You are interested in one person, not in life." Like Fowler who finally is led to take a side in the Vietnam conflict by his love for Phuong and by his witnessing the murder of innocent people, Wormwold, through the love of his daughter and his sense of responsibility for the murder of his best friend, recognizes that loyalty must extend beyond one individual. He thus avenges his friend's murder and later plans to marry Beatrice.

What sets *Our Man in Havana* apart from the earlier pieces is Greene's development of an important new theme, described by John Atkins as "the growing insistence that life resembles a dream, that our dreams may be our inner convictions, that dream logic is the significant logic."[5] In this respect, *Our Man in Havana* most closely resembles *Travels with My Aunt* and *Monsignor Quixote* where, Greene argues, the borders between fact and fiction, reality and illusion, are indiscernible.

James Wormwold can be seen as a man who discovers the powers of dreaming and creation. This "fairy story" opens with Dr. Hasselbacher and Wormwold enjoying a drink together in the Wonder Bar. The shadow of Lewis Carroll's Wonderland is further extended in Dr. Hasselbacher's advice to his friend: "You should dream more, Mr. Wormwold. Reality in our century is not something to be faced." Through his subsequent creation of characters and reports, Wormwold establishes his own Wonderland and in essence becomes an author in whom dream and reality blend together as one. Milly asks him, "Are you becoming a writer?" To which he replies, "Yes—an imaginative writer." The death of the reconaissance pilot, Raul, marks the point at which fiction and reality merge. Wormwold's question, "Can we write human beings into existence?" is to be answered in the affirmative, and anticipates Monsignor Quixote's pantomime mass during which he administers the "fictional" but no less real Host to the mayor. Wormwold's fiction encompasses the actual world and thus brings about Raul's and Dr. Hasselbacher's deaths and the attempt on his own life. All of these events are set in motion through the imaginative powers of the naive author. It is interesting to note, however, that Wormwold's dreaming mind was first stirred by a concern for real money. Money helps him to secure still another dream, that of Milly's happiness. Wormwold thus comes to represent the creative artist who consumes reality for his fiction and in turn is nearly consumed by his own creation.

Related to this theme is the recurrent figure of the clown. Wormwold, who admires the clown and models his own life after him, reflects on the comic role as means of survival:

The cruel come and go like cities and thrones and powers, leaving their ruins behind them. They had no permanence. But the clown whom he had seen last year with Milly at the circus—that clown was permanent, for his act never changed. That was the way to live: the clown was unaffected by the vagaries of public men and the enormous discoveries of the great.

He goes on to tell Milly that "If only we had been born clowns, nothing bad would happen to us except a few bruises and a smear of whitewash." His later involvement in the circus of espionage turns him into a clown spotlighted in center ring. After Wormwold, who "had no vocation for violence," shoots Carter's Dunhill instead of his intended victim, Carter cries out, "You—you clown," to which Greene adds, "How right Carter was."

Wormwold the clown is a survivor in his own fairy story. Obviously not the traditional fairy of folklore, Wormwold nevertheless is mischievous and capricious, and possesses the power of magic and enchantment. The clown-artist is a paradox in that he stands outside of time (where the "Reality in our century is not something to be faced") while simultaneously embodying in the art of his comic fiction the passing events of the cruel who "come and go like cities and thrones and powers."

4

ᙍᙍ

Short Stories

In the Introduction to his *Collected Stories* Greene describes his tales as "a collection of escapes from the novelist's world." The short story, he feels, allows him to escape from having to live with another character for years on end, "picking up his jealousies, his meanness, his dishonest tricks of thought, his betrayals." Whatever his motivation, Greene has produced three volumes of short stories: *Twenty-One Stories, A Sense of Reality*, and *May We Borrow Your Husband?* A number of the stories are trivial, some are sketches of characters and events for his novels, and some are clear works of art. Greene himself writes that "I believe I have never written anything better than *The Destructors, A Chance for Mr. Lever, Under the Garden, Cheap in August.*"

The first piece in *Twenty-One Stories* is a chilling account of violence entitled "The Destructors." The hero is a boy named Trevor, the son of a former architect now turned clerk. Trevor has acquired his father's keen sense of architectural splendor, but paradoxically his reaction to beauty is destructive. Having been invited into the house of an old man called Old Misery by the gang of boys Trevor belongs to, Trevor is fascinated by the antiquity and design of the house, which was built by Christopher Wren. The building is not only architecturally unique, but is also the only house left standing amid the rubble of the blitz. It has survived the Nazi bombers, but will not survive Trevor's mad plan.

Trevor gains the leadership of his gang through his outrageous plan to destroy Old Misery's house. When the old man leaves town for the weekend, the gang proceeds under Trevor's masterful supervision to remove the plumbing, wires, floors, and fixtures, so that only the walls of the building remain. Trevor achieves the status of a destructive artist directing a virtuoso performance: "Streaks of light came in through the closed shutters where they worked with the seriousness of creators—and destruction after all is a form of creation. A kind of imagination had seen this house as it had now become."

Old Misery, meanwhile, returns home unexpectedly, and Trevor for the moment "had no words as his dreams shook and slid." But he arranges to lock the old man in the lavatory located in the backyard until he completes his destruction. He ties a rope between a supporting beam of the house and a parked cab. The next morning when the cabbie drives off to work, the house comes crashing down. The driver, hearing Old Misery's shouts, releases him from the lavatory. He sobs out, "Where's my house?" and the cabbie simply laughs at the absurdity of the situation. Greene writes: "One moment the house had stood there with such dignity between the bomb-sites like a man in a top hat, and then, bang, crash, there wasn't anything left—not anything." The cabbie apologizes for his laughter but goes on to say, "There's nothing personal, but you got to admit it's funny."

Trevor is reminiscent of Pinkie, Greene's most terrifying boy villain, only there is no black humor in *Brighton Rock* as there is in this story. Further

more, there is no logical motivation for Trevor's behavior, as there is for Pinkie's; rather, his cold, cal-
culating moves appear to be directed by a blind instinct, stirred in part by his father's demotion to
clerk and by his mother's sense of superiority over
others. He represents the dark side of the artist, the
side that would annihilate the civilized world and
render the intricate designs of beauty a stunning
void.

The theme of destruction is turned inward in
"A Drive in the Country," a story that bears a strik-
ing resemblance to *Brighton Rock*. A young girl, fed
up with the meticulous regularity and materialism
of her father, plans to run away with her boyfriend
Fred. "She wanted to match the odd reckless quality
of Fred's mind" and, like Pinkie's girlfriend, Rose,
she surrenders her will to the strange and exhila-
rating events that lie ahead of her. She and Fred
drive off to the country where he surprises her by
proposing a suicide pact. "Life's hell. There's nothing we can do," he argues, and like Pinkie, "he was
like a skilled logician; he knew all the stages of the
argument." But despite his protestations of love, the
girl lacks the mad compassion and trust of Rose and
backs off. Fred, nevertheless, goes into the woods
and shoots himself. The escape from her parents and
the dangerous companionship of Fred, attractive as
they were, suddenly terrify her. She flees home with
the awareness that she "had wanted a little of both
worlds: irresponsibility and a safe love, danger and
a secure heart." The story ends with the assurance
that "she could feel nothing but gladness that she
had escaped from him" and that "She was quite free
from pain."

This story is interesting as a preliminary sketch
of Pinkie and Rose. Fred's character is vague and
his reckless desire to destroy himself and the girl

poorly motivated. The girl's refusal to trust Fred
merely underscores the shallowness of their relationship. She is fascinated with the idea of rebel-
liousness but is not herself a true rebel. By the time
he wrote *Brighton Rock* Greene had discovered the
key to the problem. He made Rose totally committed to Pinkie and allotted the need for safety and
security to Ida Arnold, a woman who enjoys a good
time but never experiences the anguish of true love.

Greene's revulsion at the human body under-
lies the theme of "A Little Place Off the Edgeware
Road." The hero is a man named Craven (suggesting
both his cowardice and recalling the character
Raven). All the way to the park, Craven "was re-
minded of passion but you needed money for love.
All that a poor man could get was lust." Craven carries his body "like something he hated" and recalls
a recurrent dream: "he had been alone in the huge
cavernous burying ground of all the world. Every
grave was connected to another under the ground:
the globe was honeycombed for the sake of the
dead, and on each occasion of dreaming he had discovered anew the horrifying fact that the body
doesn't decay." Intrigued by dreams, Greene here
portrays the ultimate Swiftian nightmare, the im-
mortalization of the human body with all of its dis-
gusting defects. Craven is repulsed at the thought
that "There are no worms and dissolution. Under
the ground the world was littered with masses of
dead flesh ready to rise again with their warts and
boils and eruptions."

When Craven enters a motion picture theater,
a small bearded man sits next to him and begins to
speak what sounds like nonsense. Piecing things together, Craven comes to realize that the man must
be the murderer in a recent tragedy he read about.
He calls the police to report the man; they inform

him that they already have the murderer in custody but that the body has disappeared. Craven remembers the sticky hand that the man laid on his leg, and he is "back in the horror of his dream—the squalid darkening street was only one of the innumerable tunnels connecting grave to grave where the imperishable bodies lay." He tries to convince himself that he is dreaming, but when he looks into a mirror he sees tiny drops of blood on his face, and he screams out, "I won't go mad. I'm sane. I won't go mad." But a crowd gathers around him, and soon a policeman comes, apparently to carry him off to an insane asylum.

The conclusion weakens this story because it is clear to the reader that Craven's view of the world is a mad and obsessive one, that he is locked into a nightmare that torments his waking life. It would have been better if Greene had ended the tale with the idea that Craven was "back in the horror of his dream." One does not really care if he is sane or not, but his nightmare about the dead and living is of considerable interest. Greene writes that "Sometimes identification with a character goes so far that one may dream his dream, and not one's own." In light of the repulsion toward sexuality repeatedly exhibited by such characters as Raven, Pinkie, and Minty, one suspects that Greene may well have dreamed the dream of Craven.

The theme of innocence, which runs through most of the stories in this volume, is the dominant theme of "I Spy," "The End of the Party," "The Innocent," and "The Basement Room." Greene describes "I Spy" as having "simplicity of language, the sense of life as it is lived." It is the story of a young boy, Charlie Stowe (whose name suggests a stowaway), who sneaks down into his father's tobacco shop late at night to smoke a cigarette. While

he is down there he sees his father, accompanied
by two strangers, enter the shop. Apparently he is
being arrested for spying but neither the reader nor
Charlie knows exactly what is happening. The masterful quality of this story lies in Greene's description of the boy's instinctive response to the mystery
that adult life now presents him: "He remembered
how his father had held tight to his collar and fortified himself with proverbs, and he thought for the
first time that, while his mother was boisterous and
kindly, his father was very like himself, doing things
in the dark which frightened him." By the skillful
use of the third-person narrator, Greene reveals just
enough information to allow the reader to partici-
pate in the boy's limited perspective, while at the
same time providing the reader with insights into
the peculiar confusion of the innocent mind faced
with love and fear.

A more melodramatic and contrived work, "The
End of the Party" deals with the subject of twins.
Francis Morton tells his brother Peter that he
dreamed he was dead. The figure of death is represented by the image of a bird, a creature that
Greene himself always feared. Francis panics at the
thought of attending a party where he will have to
play hide-and-seek because he is afraid of the dark
and senses that something bad will happen to him.
But he is forced to go, and when the children an-
nounce that they will play hide-and-seek, Peter sees
"a great bird darken his brother's face with its
wings." In order to comfort his brother, who is hiding in a corner during the game, Peter takes his
hand. Francis is so startled by the touch that he dies
of fright. Peter, too young to understand the paradox, "wondered with an obscure self-pity why it was
that the pulse of his brother's fear went on and on,
when Francis was now where he had always been

told there was no more terror and no more darkness." Through the half-open eyes of these children, then, Greene projects his own vision of the terror of life, a vision that lies at the heart of many of his mature novels.

"The Innocent" deals with the mystery of innocence that cannot be penetrated by the adult mind. The story is based on Greene's visit to Berkhamsted, the place of his birth. The narrator, accompanied by Lola, a girl he picked up, returns to his childhood home in the country. Lola, with her cheap perfume, stands in contrast to the young girl the narrator was in love with as a child. He goes to a hole in a gate where he used to leave secret messages for this girl and discovers one of his own messages still remaining there. He examines it and is shocked to find "a picture of crude obscenity." He feels betrayed and wonders if Lola is really so much out of place here after all. But later he realizes that the drawing has a "deep innocence": "I had believed I was drawing something with a meaning and beautiful; it was only now after thirty years of life that the picture seemed obscene." Like Charlie Stowe and Francis Morton, the child in this story is a fragile mystery that can only be glimpsed by an adult, but it is a tantalizing glimpse that was to set Greene off to the far corners of the uncivilized world and to the regions of fantasy in a obsessive attempt to recover the unadulterated experience of childhood simplicity, peace, and trust.

The best of this group of stories is "The Basement Room." Here Greene explores the theme of the loss of innocence and the lasting effect on a child's life of a single traumatic event. In his parents' absence Philip Lane has been left in the care of the butler and his wife, Mr. and Mrs. Baines. Seven-year-old Philip for the first time in his life enters the basement where the servants live. He "vibrated with the strange, the new experience." "This is life," he thinks, but as the story proves, it turns out to be death, both for Mrs. Baines and for his own innocence.

Philip admires Baines because he "had seen the world." He fills the boy's head with stories of his adventures in far-off and exotic places. Mrs. Baines, on the other hand, resembles the witch at the corner whom Greene once dreamed of. She is a domineering figure who nags her husband and threatens Philip. Philip, of course, does not understand the relationship between these adults, but he gets a painful insight into it one day when he discovers Baines in a restaurant with a strange girl. "He would never escape that scene" because he never understood it. "It conditioned his career, the long austerity of his life; when he was dying, rich and alone, it was said that he asked: 'Who is she?'" Baines tells him that she is his niece, but the reader knows her to be his mistress.

"Caught up in other people's darkness," Philip is now thrust into the adult world of secrets and lies as he becomes a pawn in the match between Mr. and Mrs. Baines. Philip "would have nothing to do with their secrets, the responsibilities they were determined to lay upon him." But one day Baines has the girl, Emmy, visit him when Mrs. Baines is away, and his infidelity is discovered when she returns unexpectedly. Philip is caught up in the powerful tension in the house and he protests: "It wasn't fair, the walls were down again between his world and theirs. . . ; a passion moved in the house he recognized but could not understand." And thus, "Life fell on him with savagery." Baines struggles with his wife and she falls over the banister "in a flurry of black clothes" (like a witch) to her death. The world of the nursery dies also, and "the whole house has been turned over to the grown-up world."

When the police come, Philip, exhausted by the web of secrets and lies thrown upon him, tells what he has seen and cries out that "It was all Emmy's fault." The constable asks Baines, "who is she?"— the same question that is to haunt Philip even to his deathbed. The simple, trusting, hero-worshiping mind of the child has been shattered in the dark underworld of the basement room. Philip could live happily with the bifurcation of good and evil as embodied in Mr. and Mrs. Baines respectively, but the powerful ambiguity presented in Emmy and her relationship to Baines burned deeply into Philip's mind and changed the course of his life.

"The Hint of an Explanation" is an ironic story about a young Catholic boy whose faith is strengthened by the town atheist. Like "The Basement Room," this story makes the point that a single event in a child's life can dramatically affect his future. A terrifying character named Blacker, a baker by trade, bribes the hero, a boy named David, with an electric train set if he will bring him the Communion Host. Obsessed with his atheism, Blacker wants to examine the Host to prove once and for all that Christ's body and blood are not there. Driven by his fear of Blacker and his desire for the train set, the boy goes to Communion and lodges the Host under his tongue. When he is alone, he wraps the Host in a piece of newspaper and carries it home so that he can give it to Blacker the next day. The boy for the first time begins to realize through Blacker's obsession that the Host, which he previously took for granted each Sunday, was something special indeed: "I knew that this which I had beside my bed was something of infinite value—something a man would pay for with his whole peace of mind, something that was so hated one could love it as one loves an outcast or a bullied child." And so, David swallows the Host at the last minute instead of turning it over to Blacker. "Then something happened," recalls David, now an adult, "which seemed to me now more terrible than his desire to corrupt or my thoughtless act: he began to weep."

As the story ends, David is revealed to be a priest, thereby demonstrating God's ironic providence. The demonic Blacker, filled with hatred and finally with the anguish of frustration, has led the indifferent boy into the powerful mysteries of his own religion. Greene employed this same irony in *The End of the Affair* when the atheist preacher unwittingly brings Sarah into the Catholic church.

"A Chance for Mr. Lever" is based on Greene's travels through Liberia and represents the adult's dream of peace, freedom, and home. For thirty years Mr. Lever sold heavy machinery in Europe and the United States, but now he finds himself in Africa with his home in Eastbourne only a dream. His mission is to find a man who will enable him to make a great deal of money by authorizing a contract for earth-moving equipment. Enduring the squalor and heat of the journey, he finally discovers his man, but too late, for he has just died from yellow fever. "It seemed at first to be the end of everything, of his journey, his hopes, his life with Emily." And it is the image of his wife Emily that continues to sustain him through his ordeal. Like so many of Greene's heroes, Mr. Lever requires one personal relationship to give meaning and shape to his life, and now even that is threatened.

Suddenly all of Mr. Lever's conventional views are undermined by his awareness of mortality. Pondering the solemnity of death, he asserts that "death wasn't solemn: it was a lemon-yellow skin and a black vomit." All of the moral clichés of his past, such as "Honesty is the best policy," lose their meaning. Only his devotion to his wife moves him now: he and she must survive, so he forges a letter from the dead man ordering a shipment of the heavy machinery. Mr. Lever has won. He will be wealthy now and can return home to Eastbourne to live happily with Emily. He is free at last from the restraints that held him through a long and unrewarding career. The reader discovers in the last paragraph, however, that the mosquito that bit the dead man has also bitten Mr. Lever and that along with the forgery he carries back with him through the jungle he also carries the fatal dose of yellow fever. A kindly god, if there is a god, the narrator says, "was ready to give Mr. Lever three days of happiness, three days off the galling chain" before he died.

Thus the African jungle becomes an ironic place of innocence for the hero. He has found the mystical peace and joy of childhood that Querry sought in Pendélé, only it is imaginary, a mirage that the reader knows will soon vanish as a result of a mere mosquito bite. Happiness, like innocence, is at best a dream for the adult, and one's attempt to capture it results in anguish or self-deception.

In retrospect, *Twenty-One Stories* explores the subject of the irrevocable loss of innocence and the paradoxical quest of man for the lost child that haunts his dreams. It is interesting to note, however, that the world of experience is usually presented in terms of a nightmare: Trevor's destruction of the historical house, Craven's dream of the uncorrupted dead, or Fred's suicide pact in the woods. In this dark world, life is the embodiment of horror and terror. One can flee from it, like Fred, by taking his own life, or one can, like Philip, carry the mystery of innocence within oneself, suffering from its trou-

bling hints of what was once and can never be again.
None of these characters can ever again be truly free
from his past, and the stories clearly demonstrate
William Wordsworth's statement that "The Child is
Father to the Man."

The most interesting tale in *A Sense of Reality*
is the long story entitled "Under the Garden."
Gwenn Boardman accurately describes it as "a
mythic rendition of [Greene's] recurrent theme of
lost childhood, of a universal 'journey without
maps,' and a quest for 'the heart of the matter,' enriched by episodes, characters, and symbols made
familiar in earlier contexts."[1]

The hero, William Wilditch, returns to the
scene of his boyhood vacations in an attempt to recover a childhood memory that took root there. He
remembers having spent three days and nights
(though his practical and antipoetic mother claims
he was actually gone only a few hours) in a strange
world under the garden. The narrator enters the garden and recreates the tantalizing and mysterious
dream of his youth.

Obviously influenced by Lewis Carroll's *Alice's Adventures in Wonderland*, Greene has his
hero enter a bizarre underground world where conventional reality and logic are challenged by Javitt,
the ruler of this realm. A white-bearded, dirty old
man sitting on a lavatory seat, Javitt delights in playing with logic and language, and his mind suggests
that of the Mad Hatter or Humpty Dumpty. "You
can call me Javitt," he tells Wilditch, "but only because it's not my real name." He then asks the boy,
"If you had a dog named Jupiter, you wouldn't believe he was really Jupiter, would you?" Like
Humpty-Dumpty, Javitt enjoys confusing the child
with puns. When Wilditch reads in a newspaper an

announcement of a garden fête, Javitt asks, "Was it a good fate or an evil fate?"

Javitt's view of his world is novel, vigorous, and paradoxical. "Be disloyal," he advises the boy, "it's your duty to the human race. . . . The same applies to women and God. They both respect a man they don't own." It becomes quickly apparent that Javitt is a spokesman for the childlike imagination that is required to be a successful writer, an imagination that must be preserved and nurtured in an adult world that emphasizes practicality and conventional thinking.

Wilditch himself resembles Greene in his journeys without maps, his search for the lost simplicity of childhood that lead him into the jungles of Africa and South America. Wilditch remarks that half the time "I only wanted to laugh freely and happily at the strangeness of [Javitt's] speech and the novelty of his ideas." Seated on his seedy "throne," Javitt embodies the ars poetica expressed in Greene's own writings, and his realm is redolent of *King Solomon's Mines*, Berkhamsted, Pendélé, and Liberia.

There is another component, however, to the child's fantasy vision besides that of the freedom, laughter, and joy of creativity—and that is fear. Javitt's servant-companion, Maria, is a grotesque old woman in dirty sequined clothes with hands "curved like a bird's." The only sound this threatening figure can produce is "Kwahk." She is the recurrent nightmare creature—"the witch at the corner"—that haunted Greene's youth and later fiction. She is Mrs. Baines in a purer form of the grotesque. If Javitt represents the creative imagination, then Maria symbolizes the terror of life, a twisted form of the human dimension that creates a basic horror and threatens death. She is the dark force that gives the dramatic and ironic impact to Greene's heroes' desperate search for peace and happiness.

There is no mortality under the garden, even as no one dies once he or she is translated into a work of fiction. Life is sustained through the dream of the creative mind. As Wilditch comes to realize, "Absolute reality belongs to dreams and not to life," and this observation is implicit throughout Greene's fiction, including his most recent novel, *Monsignor Quixote.*

The effect of the childhood dream on Wilditch is to lead him to live a restless, unconventional life, always searching for the concealed ghost of his childhood: "If it had not been for his dream of the tunnel and the bearded man and the hidden treasure, couldn't he have made a less restless life for himself, as George [his brother] had done, with marriage, children, a home?" As Greene's own life clearly demonstrates, the hidden treasure that obsessed Wilditch has also lured him into the life of a wanderer seeking his buried life.

And so, Greene creates in "Under the Garden" a quasi-allegory of his own development as a novelist. Like Wilditch, he can trace his creativity to his obsession with the joys and terrors of childhood, profound experiences that have shaped and controlled his career as a writer and made the significance of dreams paramount as the language of ultimate reality. Like Lewis Carroll, Greene recognizes that out of the fantasies of childhood arise the true and often terrorizing dreams of the adult artist.

Set in Sweden, "Dream of a Strange Land" is the story of a man who has contracted leprosy while in Africa and who is desperate to receive private treatment for his disease in order to avoid having his life made even more miserable through public disclosure of his illness at a hospital. The old professor of medicine who has been treating him now says that he can no longer continue to do so and that the patient must enter a hospital. Shortly after the patient leaves, the professor's house is transformed into a gambling casino for one night in order to entertain a senile general. When the leper returns that night to make a final plea for treatment, he discovers the bizarre metamorphosis: "The patient stood motionless in the snow, with his face pressed to the glass, and he thought, The wrong house? But this is not the wrong house; it is the wrong country. He felt that he could never find his way home from here—it was too far away." When the champagne corks are popped, a faint explosion is heard outside the house, the leper apparently having committed suicide.

Reminiscent of Querry in *A Burnt-Out Case*, the patient is the familiar Greene outcast looking in on a society that seems fabricated, unreal, and one that he knows he can never rejoin. His "home" is as far away and unreachable as Querry's Pendélé, and only death will bring an end to his suffering.

The rest of the stories in *A Sense of Reality* range across a number of subjects. "A Visit to Morin" is a semiautobiographical account of a famous Catholic novelist who acknowledges that he has lost his belief but not his faith. He stays away from the sacraments because "if I returned and they failed me, then I would really be a man without faith." "The Church Militant" and "The Blessing" are slight pieces also dealing with the Catholic church. The former is about a group of missionary nuns who come to work in a dangerous part of Africa. "The Blessing" presents the paradoxical theme that "We have to bless what we hate." "Dear Dr. Falkenheim" exhibits Greene's black humor. It is the story of a young boy's trauma upon seeing Father Christmas beheaded by a helicopter blade. Ironically, the man's death convinces the boy of the reality of Father Christmas. "Of course he's real," the boys exclaims, "I saw him die."

Even when Greene sets his story in the distant future, as in "A Discovery in the Woods," he asserts the familiar theme of lost innocence. It is an account of an isolated race of small, deformed people living after an atomic blast. A group of children explore the woods around their village and discover a skeleton. One of the boys looks down at his own stunted and uneven legs, and the girl next to him begins to "keen again for a whole world lost." The boy marvels at the discovery lying at their feet: "He's six feet tall and he has beautiful straight legs." As in "The Basement Room" the adults are the villains who warp the sensibilities of the young. This time the adults have destroyed the secret garden of childhood with the ultimate weapons of destruction instead of with lies and secrets.

A much more uneven collection than *Twenty-One Stories*, *A Sense of Reality* nevertheless extends and develops Greene's insistent theme of the lost world, and in "Under the Garden" he works out for the first time a mythological parable of his own art. Most of the stories in these two volumes are serious, searching, and dreamlike attempts to come to grips with Greene's obsession with childhood, innocence, fear, and terror. The next volume, however, turns to the lighter and sadly comic side of life.

May We Borrow Your Husband? was written, according to Greene, "in a single mood of sad hilarity, while I was establishing a home in a two-roomed apartment over the port in Antibes." The setting for many of the stories is Antibes, and the narrator is often an observant writer who, like Greene, overhears the tales of the strange lives going on about him.

Three of the stories deal with homosexuality. In the title story two interior decorators, Tony and Stephen, try to seduce a young man away from his new bride during the couple's honeymoon. They manipulate the narrator to entertain the bride while they drive off with her husband. At the end of the story she naively announces that Tony will visit them in London for several months in order to decorate their house. Greene depicts Tony and Stephen as cruel, witty, and self-indulgent creatures who hunt their prey with the cunning of animals. He extends his dislike of homosexuals in "Chagrin in Three parts," in which a lesbian named Madame Desjoie seduces Madame Volet shortly after her husband deserts her. "Two Gentle People" continues with this theme of sexual disappointments by recording the brief encounter of a man and woman who realize that they might be happy together, but because they are already married they return to their ordinary lives—he to a dumb American girl named Patience and she to a husband engaged in a homosexual relationship with a stranger.

These three tales exhibit an aura of decadence and concealed bitterness at the waste of female sexuality in the sophisticated and exotic world of Antibes. There is a rich irony in the final comment of the narrator of "Chagrin in Three Parts" when he says of Madame Volet: "I was glad that she was in the kind reliable hands of Madame Desjoie." One recalls the pathetic attachments of Mabel Warren in *Stamboul Train*.

Some of the other stories deal with different abnormalities. "The Over-night Bag," for example, is about a man who carries a mysterious bag that contains, he claims, his wife's dead baby. "A Shocking Incident" is a piece of black humor about a boy who discovers that his father was killed when a pig fell from a balcony and landed on him. And "Doctor Crombie" presents a physician who claims that sexual intercourse causes cancer. They are trivial works, however, and require no comment.

Greene's finest piece of writing in this collection is "Cheap in August," a surprisingly tender and compassionate story in light of the cruelty and superficiality of the stories that surround it. An Englishwoman named Mary Watson is on vacation in Jamaica because it is "cheap in August." Although she loves her American husband, an English professor, who is at home working on a study of James Thomson's "The Seasons," she decides that she wants to have an affair, an adventure. She quickly discovers, however, "the essential morality of a holiday resort in the cheap season; there were no opportunities for infidelity, only for writing postcards."

Thirty-nine years old, she feels it is absurd not to be content, but her restlessness is not due simply to physical desires, she argues, but represents "the universal desire to see a bit further, before one surrendered to old age and the blank certitude of death." As fate would have it, she is soon involved in the most unlikely, bizarre affair, one she never planned but that profoundly affects her life.

At the swimming pool she meets an American named Henry Hickslaughter. Greene describes him as "a solitary elephant," an old man with "rolls of fat folding over the blue bathing-slip." They have lunch together, and before long Mary "began to feel oddly at ease with the old man." In a way, Henry is like herself. He came to Jamaica because it is cheap in August, and he appears lonely and unfulfilled, and with little time in life remaining to find happiness. That evening she goes to his room for a drink, and they discuss a variety of subjects, from Longfellow to their family lives. They then go down for dinner, after which he invites her back to his room because, as he says, "I don't sleep well." She refuses at first, afraid that perhaps even at his age Henry might have some sexual designs on her. These thoughts make her feel ignoble, however, and she feels unjustified in refusing him a half-hour's companionship; and so, she goes to his room with a bottle of sleeping pills to help him sleep.

When she enters she is startled to find him crying. "I wanted company," he says, and she reassures him. He admits that he is afraid of being alone and that he would have paid the maid to stay with him if necessary. At this point Henry is no longer described as an elephant but as a geographical region to be explored and marveled at: "It was as if she were discovering for the first time the interior of the enormous continent on which she had elected to live." The stereotyped American turns out to have a tender soul, scarred by failure and dread. "But here, stretched on the bed . . . failure and fear talked to her without shame, and in an American accent. It was as though she were living in the remote future, after God knew what catastrophe."

Like an anxious and troubled child soothed by his mother, Henry finally falls asleep. Mary lies on the bed beside him outside the sheet, and he is lying away from her so that their bodies do not touch. But filled with pity and compassion she arouses his sexuality, and they make love. She feels no guilt but

weeps a little at the temporary nature of this meeting. And when "His body began to slip out of
her, . . . it was as if he were carrying away her unknown child, in the direction of Curaçao, and she
tried to hold him back, the fat old frightened man
whom she almost loved."

On one level this story makes one think of
Henry as Greene himself, in need of a loving
younger woman to reassure and comfort him in a
terrifyingly impersonal world. Over and over again
Greene has presented heroes, such as Fowler, Scobie, and Castle, with similar needs. There is also an
ironic sense of sexuality and motherhood fused in
the women of these works; the men are old enough
to be fathers to the women but they frequently present themselves as frightened children who need
these females to comfort and nurture them.

There is a wonderful innocence about Henry.
The fact that he is an American is important, for
Greene has frequently presented the American as
an innocent but never so sympathetically. The
Smiths in *The Comedians* are well-meaning fools
and Alden Pyle in *The Quiet American* is unthink-
ingly cruel, but Henry Hickslaughter, despite his
name, is vulnerable, tender, and compassionate. He
is the lost child seeking a home and never really
finding it, except for the brief encounter in Jamaica.
He is the unknown child who irrevocably slips away
from Mary. She has discovered America and lost it
in the same night.

In his short stories, then, Greene has shown us
children without innocence, such as Trevor and the
children in "A Discovery in the Woods" and adults
who embody innocence, such as Henry Hickslaughter and William Wilditch. Many of these stories are
very contrived or self-conscious escapes from real-

ity, but several of them—such as "The Destructors,"
"I Spy," "The Basement Room," "A Hint of an Explanation," "Under the Garden," and "Cheap in August"—stand in relationship to the others as
Greene's novels do to his entertainments.

5

〰〰〰〰〰〰〰〰〰〰〰〰〰〰〰〰〰〰〰〰〰〰〰〰〰〰〰〰

Plays

Besides writing novels, short stories, film criticism, travel books, and essays, Greene also wrote five plays, all of which were successfully produced and popularly received. Greene's reputation as a novelist, combined with the excellent acting of such great professionals as Eric Portman (as Father Brown in *The Living Room*), John Gielgud (as James Callifer in *The Potting Shed*), Ralph Richardson (as Victor Rhodes in *The Complaisant Lover* and the Father in *Carving a Statue*), and Paul Scofield (as Clive Root in *The Complaisant Lover*), helped to attract a great deal of contemporary critical attention to his plays. But over the years they have fallen into relative obscurity, almost completely overshadowed by his work in the novel. Old-fashioned, quaint, and occasionally soporific in their extended philosophical and religious discussions, these plays nevertheless afford an interesting comparison to Greene's novels. They present characters and themes that reappear more convincingly in his fiction, and so, one can see in these plays the early drafts of his novels.

The Living Room employs the ménage à trois that appears in many of Greene's novels, such as *The Heart of the Matter* and *The End of the Affair*. As in those works, the central conflict of this play revolves around a character's attempt to do what is nearly impossible: enjoy a love affair within the context of a strict Roman Catholic theology.

Rose Pemberton (her name recalls the suicide of the innocent young man with the same last name in *The Heart of the Matter*) comes to live with her great aunts, Teresa and Helen Browne, after the death of her mother. These two women are devout, indeed, pious Catholics, who care for their brother James, a priest, paralyzed from the waist down as a result of an auto accident. The Brownes have closed up all the rooms in which their ancestors died, and so the living room in which all of the action of the play takes place, assumes a symbolic significance.

When Helen, who rules the Browne household, discovers that Rose is having an affair with a married man, Michael Dennis, she keeps her from running off with him by making Teresa ill, thereby calling up Rose's pity and sense of responsibility. Despite her Catholic background, Rose is willing to live with Dennis until one day Dennis's wife confronts her and, for the first time, she sees her as a real person. After this very emotional scene, Michael, overwhelmed by a renewed sense of pity for his wife, follows after her. Tormented by grief, Rose seeks the advice of Father James, but his platitudes fail to comfort or sustain her, and she commits suicide in the living room. The conclusion shows Teresa asserting herself against Helen's superstition by making her bed in the living room, thereby rejecting Helen's fear of death and suggesting her faith in a merciful God.

The plot is reminiscent of *The Heart of the Matter*, only Greene has transferred Rose's Catholicism and suicide to Scobie. Michael's willingness to leave his wife and his easily assuaged conscience make him a much less interesting and intense character than Scobie. Unlike the novel, however, this play reads more like a religious tract than a drama about actual people.

The great advantage that Greene has in his novels is that the narrator can suggest religious and philosophical problems without seeming contrived and pompous. The characters in his plays, however, become insufferable when they begin discussing theology. Father James, for example, has a dual role in that he articulates a theology that fails to solve Rose's problem but which, at the same time, underscores the play's theme that God is merciful. He says such things as "Mercy is what I believe in," and after Rose's death he argues that one should not assume she is damned, for only God knows her final state of mind. He suggests that now that she has borne her "child," pain, God has forgiven her sins. The spokesman for the church, Father James, thus fails to save Rose from suicide with his various platitudes, such as his counsel to pray. Nevertheless, we are expected to believe this ineffectual priest when he tells the family that everything will turn out all right in eternity. It is not very satisfying for the audience to witness Rose's psychological and spiritual breakdown and the failure of the church to help her, and then be told that, like Humpty-Dumpty, she will be put back together again by a merciful God.

The trouble with Greene's stage Catholics is that they wear their Catholicism like stiff new clothes: they look a bit silly, are clearly uncomfortable, and spend too much time talking about the fit. At one point in the play Rose pleads with Father James, "please say something that's not Catholic," a plea the reader might justifiably make to Greene himself in *The Living Room*.

Like the previous play, *The Potting Shed* has a symbolic title, includes a priest, involves a suicide, and opens with a death that brings together a disparate family. The Callifers have gathered at the news that old Mr. Callifer, a once prominent author of rationalist tracts, is about to die. But the family was careful to exclude two of its members from the group, old Callifer's younger son James and James's uncle, William, who defected from the rationalist tradition by converting to Catholicism and becoming a priest.

Callifer's granddaughter, Anne, allows the action to go forward by telegraphing James, inviting him to the gathering, and later by bringing in Mrs. Potter, the wife of the family's gardener, who explains the mystery lying at the heart of the play. An impish and outspoken thirteen-year-old, although an unconvincing character herself, Anne functions as a Puckish figure arranging the necessary confrontations.

The central mystery of the play centers on the symbolic potting shed, a place filled with seeds and bulbs, a place of rebirth. Something had happened there years ago that caused both James and his uncle William to become family outcasts. James's mother will not allow him to see his father before he dies, nor will she discuss the potting shed. Anne, however, invites Mrs. Potter to the house, and Mrs. Potter reveals to James that when he was a boy he hanged himself in the potting shed. Mr. Potter cut him down and saw that he was dead. Then James's uncle, William, arrived and through an apparent miracle brought him back to life.

Hearing this, James tracks down his uncle to ask what happened that day in the shed. He discovers that William has become an alcoholic, ineffectual priest who has lost his faith but who nevertheless carries out the duties and rituals of his office. Father William explains to James that he loved him as a boy and when he found him dead he prayed to God, "Take away my faith, but let him live." God answered the prayer, miraculously restoring James to life at the expense of William's faith. And since that day William, now a hollow man, has busied himself with the empty routines of the priesthood, serving a God in whom he can no longer believe.

James's self-knowledge is now complete. While he believed in nothing before, he now is totally committed to a belief in God and to a belief in the miracle of his own resurrection. The final irony of the play is Mrs. Callifer's admission that her husband was a fraudulent rationalist. He knew about the happening in the potting shed, and it convinced him that God does exist. By then his reputation as a rationalist was well established, however, and it was too late to recall all his books and begin again. His wife continued to protect his reputation by concealing her husband's conversion and by repudiating James and Father William.

The element of mystery sustains the reader's curiosity as Anne, detectivelike, helps to bring the pieces of the puzzle for James to put together. The well-constructed plot is a hallmark of Greene's fiction, and this story line is reminiscent of *The End of the Affair* with its Lazarus theme. Sarah Miles's prayer, however, is more believable than that of Father William. Her love for Bendrix and her guilt over her adulterous affair with him made her vow to give him up if God restored his life, and this is an understandable bargain. It seems very contrived, though, for a priest to offer to sacrifice his faith for a similar miracle. The bargain sounds too much like a parody of Greene enjoying putting God on the spot rather than the plea of a desperate man who deeply loves his nephew.

In any event, the characters of James and Father William are wonderfully drawn. John Atkins best summarizes the psychological emptiness of James when he writes that "He is Pyle, he is Querry, each with a difference, but most of all he is the little boy from the Basement Room who has now grown up."[1] He is, however, much more interesting as a hollow man than he is as a convert. Greene is simply better at describing the psychological and spiritual drifter than he is at portraying the fulfilled man. Father William, the zombielike priest, is another case in point. After the motion pictures in which Bing Crosby and Barry Fitzgerald played heartwarming clerics, it is refreshing to discover a character like Father William, surrounded by grotesque religious pictures in a dark, shabby room, drinking to forget his lack of faith, but keenly aware that he is "condemned to being a Father for life." But despite Father William's overwhelming sense of failure, the audience realizes that he is indeed the spiritual father to James, having brought him back from the dead in the magical potting shed.

Greene's next play, *The Complaisant Lover*, is a comedy written in the same mood of sad hilarity as were the stories in *May We Borrow Your Husband?* It presents a love triangle involving a dentist named Victor Rhodes, his wife Mary, and Clive Root, an antiquarian bookseller who is in love with Mary. Beneath the comic surface of the play there is the serious theme of domestic versus romantic love. Married for sixteen years, Mary loves Victor and their two children, and has become more or less resigned to the lack of sexual and romantic love in her marriage. Clive Root, however, offers her the excitement of an adulterous affair, and to force Mary to make a decision between him and her husband, he informs Victor of their relationship.

Victor observes: "It's unfair, isn't it, that we're only dressed for a domestic comedy," and instead of committing suicide ("A suicide looks better in a toga") to make his wife's decision easier, he decides that since there are three parties involved in this matter each must choose to be a "complaisant lover." He and Mary will continue with their normal way of life, and Clive will continue to enjoy a occasional meeting with Mary. Thus Mary loses neither her past sixteen years with Victor nor her future with Clive, though Clive believes that their continued familiarity will domesticate their romantic love and cause Mary to leave him.

A number of Greene's serious works focus on characters who, like Mary Rhodes, desire to eat their cake and have it, too. But unlike Mary, such characters as Rose Pemberton, Sarah Miles, and Scobie are forced to make agonizing decisions. Their domestic centers of gravity are strong, but their passions are stronger still and pull them into the area of tragedy. According to Victor, Mary needs the romantic illusion "That she'll love someone for the rest of her life." Her marriage, however, is firmly rooted in the thousands of mundane family details that have accumulated between Victor and herself during the past sixteen years. As she explains to Clive, "What you and I talk about is so different. With Victor I talk about Sally's room which needs re-painting . . . And then there's the dinner that went wrong. Clive, that's the sort of talk that kills desire. Only kindness grows in that soil."

The moral of this comedy suggests that domestic love and kindness are not easily exchanged for the passions and romance of adultery. Clive Root turns out to be no more harmful to Mary's marriage than would her reading of a romantic novel. Had she been a compulsive or, better still, a neurotic woman, instead of a bright, commonsensical, loving person, the play would have taken a tragic turn. It is a credit to Greene's versatility as a writer that he can see the comedy in love as well as the pain.

Carving a Statue is Greene's most innovative play and stands apart from his other productions. There is very little plot, most of the characters are universalized through their anonymity (the cast comprises The Father, His Son, The First Girl, The Second Girl, and Dr. Parker), and the action and dialogue suggest a dreamlike, symbolic atmosphere rather than the actual world. A study of an obsessive artist, the play embodies the theme of Robert Browning's "Andrea del Sarto": "Ah, but a man's reach should exceed his grasp, / Or what's a heaven for?"

The hero of the play, the Father, is a sculptor who is working on his massive rendition of God the Father. The project, which he has been working on for fifteen years, obsesses him like a maddening dream. No matter how hard he tries, he can never get the figure quite right, and since he is growing old, he senses that he may never complete his dream. His vision isolates him from his son and the rest of the world. No one has any idea of the dimensions of his romantic dream, which compels him to work out of the terrible loneliness of his own soul.

Through the character of the Father, Greene suggests that the artist is like a child, filled with wonder, moved by dreams, and incapable of dealing with the real world. When the Father's wife died, for example, he literally ran away rather than face the problem. He remembers her simply as one of his models for the Virgin. High up on his ladder shaping the face of God, the artist has little to do with the actual world.

The distance between the Father and God the Father is paralleled by the distance between the Father and his Son. Throughout the play the Father only occasionally hears what his Son is saying. An innocent like his Father, though without his years, the Son is a victim of his Father's obsession. He attempts to assert himself through a sexual encounter with a girl he brings into the studio, but the Father has sex with her instead. Later, the Son falls in love with a deaf-mute, but she gets run down by a car after Dr. Parker, the Father's physician, attempts to seduce her. Pleading with his Father as if he were God himself, the boy begs for his help, but the Father replies that he has his own work to complete. After his Son attempts to commit suicide, the Father explains to him that he can only live life at second-hand, that as long as he works he can hold away the pain of the world.

The play ends with the Father's recognition that he will never recreate God the Father, but his artistic hope is renewed with another obsession, a new idea. Instead of the love of God the Father he turns his interest toward the infernal pride of Lucifer. And so, if the artist cannot encompass God in his works, Greene suggests, then perhaps he can try to recreate Lucifer, someone closer to home.

The obliqueness of this work opens it up to a variety of possible interpretations, but an obvious and fundamental reading is that it is about Greene's own obsession as a writer, his compulsive attempt to formulate in words his paradoxical vision of a world torn by the conflict between good and evil, innocence and experience, the ideal and the actual. Furthermore, the creative artist can more easily bear

the pain of this world if he sees it, as the Father
says, "second-hand," through such characters as
Raven, the whisky priest, and Scobie. The death of
his wife , the anguish of his young son, and his own
unfulfilled dream quite naturally turn the Father's
chisel toward the face of Lucifer, the powerful
demon who haunts and inspires the nightmare
world of Greene's own fiction.

Greene's latest play, *The Return of A. J. Raffles*,
is an Edwardian comedy loosely based on the characters in Ernest William Hornung's novel *The Am-
ateur Cracksman*. The brother-in-law of Arthur
Conan Doyle, Hornung created Raffles as a counterpart to the more intellectual Sherlock Holmes.
Inspired by Hornung's books, Greene began work
on his play shortly after seeing the Royal Shakespeare Company's production of *Sherlock Holmes*
in 1974.

Greene's farce is the story of A. J. Raffles, a
gentleman burglar who, with his homosexual accomplice Bunny, breaks into the home of the Mar-
quis of Queensberry. Lord Alfred Douglas, angry at
his father for stopping his allowance after his scandalous affair with Oscar Wilde, puts the two refined
burglars up to this caper. Past their prime now, these
charming thieves manage to steal only a gold box
and some compromising letters written by Bertie,
the Prince of Wales, to his mistress. Worse than that,
however, they get caught. But Bertie is so taken with
Raffles's military record—he was wounded in the
battle of Spion Kop during the Boer War—and by
his skill at cricket—he helped to beat the Austra-
lians in 1896—that he gets the charges against him
and Bunny dropped. Advising Raffles to retire from
burglary, the good-hearted prince leaves, and Raf-

fles tells Bunny that the Prince will become a great
king if he lives long enough.

The Prince of Wales's scandalous love affairs
and extravagant living were an embarrassment to
the queen and an affront to the strict moral code of
the Victorians. The Edwardian age, to which he
gave his name, also acquired a reputation for its
loose morals and decadence. As if they heard the
thunder of the approaching world war, many adults
shed their responsibilities to become like children
again, acting out the final play of innocence.

Filled with witty dialogue, disguises, and wry
humor, this quaint play takes some liberties with
historical fact but captures the atmosphere and character of the turn of the century. It is interesting that
Greene chose to write a play set in Edwardian times
because that is the age that belongs to his parents,
the period of his childhood memories. The play itself reflects the innocence of the period. Raffles,
Bunny, and Bertie resemble children in their care-
free exploits and playful sexuality. In a sense, *The
Return of A. J. Raffles* is Greene's wistful tribute to
a fantasy past that enshrines the adventures of a
group of aristocratic adults (a class, incidentally, to
which Greene seems to have aspired but into which
he was never fully admitted because of his background and inferior public school education) who
are unencumbered by guilt or a sense of responsibility. As Bertie explains to Raffles, it is necessary
to pretend in order to be real.

Aware of the grave reality of growing German
military might, Bertie resembles Shakespeare's
Prince Hal, a man who appears totally committed
to the enjoyment of women and drink but who will
one day, as Raffles observes, be a "great king." Still,

the central consciousness of the play reflects the
freedom, fantasy, and energy of youth. Bertie acknowledges the fragile innocence of the period
when he remarks to Raffles that they both belong
to a unique moment in history.

6

Conclusion

The achievement of Graham Greene is difficult to assess. He is a complete man of letters, having written twenty-four novels and entertainments, several volumes of short stories, five plays, a two-volume autobiography, three travel books, numerous literary and political essays, hundreds of film and book reviews, a biography of Lord Rochester, four children's books, and ten screenplays. He also has edited *British Dramatists* (1942), *The Best of Saki* (1950), *The Spy's Bedside Book* (1957), *The Bodley Head Ford Madox Ford* (1962), *Victorian Detective Fiction* (1966), and *An Impossible Woman, the Memories of Dottoressa Moor of Capri* (1975).

Despite the variety of literary forms that Greene has explored, his greatness clearly lies in his fiction. Unlike other writers of the 1920s and 1930s, he has practically ignored the experimental novel. Rather, he has followed the loose tradition of such diverse writers as Charles Dickens, Wilkie Collins, Robert Louis Stevenson, Rider Haggard, Joseph Conrad, Henry James, Ford Madox Ford, François Mauriac, and Marjorie Bowen. Greene's main achievements in the novel are two: (1) he is a master storyteller, one of the chief reasons for his popular success; (2) he has created a unique vision of the world, having turned his obsessions into works of art. Greene both lives and writes on "the dangerous edge of things," and in the world of his novels he has recreated the bittersweet conflict between the fascination of innocence and the hell-haunted drama of human existence.

Greene's exciting, fast-paced narratives have an illusive transparency about them, as if one can see and hear the characters and visualize their surroundings without the distractions of the author's presence or stylistic mannerisms. This authorial invisibility may derive from Greene's experience in writing film scripts and from the many years he spent in reviewing motion pictures. It is interesting to note in this connection how few of his novels or entertainments are written from the first person point of view, a perspective clearly unsuited to a motion picture script.

Although many of his novels are based on topical events—whether in London, Mexico, Vietnam, or Haiti—Greene's personal involvement in those events as a reporter and student of human nature allows him the perspective of an insider. And so, in his novels it is almost as if he would not ask his characters to do or think something that he himself had not done or thought. Life to Greene is a series of risks and moral choices; the dangers are betrayal, corruption, and failure. The central quest of his obsessed heroes is for the peace and innocence of their lost childhood, an adventure that is characterized by great tension and suffering, and one that ends often only in death.

Greene has the distinction allotted to few authors of being a popular writer who has the respect of the literary establishment. Some critics, however, believe that a writer with popular appeal cannot be a serious artist. In Greene's early novels he deals with this very issue through the characters of Quin

Savory, the cockney novelist, who hopes to "bring back cheerfulness and 'ealth to modern fiction"; Maurice Bendrix, who imagines his literary ranking to be "a little above (Somerset) Maugham because Maugham is popular"; and Rollo Martins. Speaking to a group of literary snobs, Martins acknowledges that an important influence on his writing is Zane Grey, to which someone replies, "He was just a popular entertainer." Furious with this patronizing remark, Martins snaps back, "Why the hell not? . . . What was Shakespeare?"

Thus Greene defends the popular novelist while at the same time worrying about his reputation among serious critics. His classification of his fiction into novels and entertainments reflects this worry and seems to say, defensively, that some of his stories he simply tossed off for popular consumption, but that the others are serious novels worthy of serious critical judgment. It is as if he solves the conflict between popularity and artistic integrity by assuming the guise of two writers: the author of thrillers for the masses, in the tradition of Rider Haggard and Robert Louis Stevenson, and the author of important novels that examine the complexities of human psychology for a more sophisticated audience, in the tradition of Joseph Conrad and Henry James. In fact, before he came up with the term "entertainment," Greene had toyed with the idea of publishing his early work under an assumed name as a means of protecting his future reputation.

Much has been written about Greene's Catholicism. While there is no question that his religion plays an important part in his writing, it proved to be a powerful distraction to literary critics of the 1950s and 1960s. By now, however, the novelty and shock of his whisky priest have passed, and the theological implications of Scobie's death no longer

call forth detailed analyses. From an artistic stand-
point one of the central functions of Catholicism in
Greene's writings is to structure the judgments and
decisions of his characters and to make them more
dramatic figures. When Scobie receives Communion in the state of mortal sin, for example, he knows,
according to the strict teachings of the church, that
he is risking the eternal damnation of his soul. Similarly, the whisky priest and Father Callifer bargain
with their souls in order to persuade God to help
someone else. Greene enjoys pressing Catholic
teachings to extraordinary limits in order to make
the lives of his characters more intensely exciting.

This is not to say that Greene uses his religion
for mere effect; rather, his characters are extensions
of his own compulsive need to cross dangerous frontiers, both physical and psychological ones, and the
demanding faith of Catholicism just happens to be
one of those frontiers. On the other hand, the Catholicism of Greene's characters, with the possible
exception of the whisky priest, has a self-conscious-
ness about it that one does not see in the writings
of someone like James Joyce. Greene's Catholicism
seems more studied and less visceral than Joyce's.
Greene's Catholics dramatize their religious beliefs,
but Joyce's embody them.

In the last analysis, Greene will merit his fame
as one of the best novelists in the twentieth century
and will be recognized, according to his wishes, as
"a writer who happens to be a Catholic." He has
left us a complex and variegated world, haunted by
the violent ghosts of Pinkie Brown and Raven on
the one hand, and by the comic and loving spirits
of James Wormwold and Father Quixote on the
other. It is a surprising, suspenseful, frightening,

and dark world, but it is above all a human place, peopled with sad and suffering men and women with a profound longing for peace, some of whom occasionally startle us with their compassion and love and childlike simplicity.

Notes

1. THE MAN AND HIS WORK

1. A. J. Liebling, "Talkative Something-or-Other," *New Yorker*, April 7, 1956, pp. 148–54.

2. NOVELS

1. Laurence Lerner, "Graham Greene," *The Critical Quarterly* V (Autumn 1963), 221.
2. Morton Dauwen Zabel, *Craft and Character in Modern Fiction* (New York: Viking, 1957), p. 282.
3. Seán O'Faoláin, "Graham Greene: 'I Suffer, Therefore I Am,'" *The Vanishing Hero: Studies in the Novelists of the Twenties* (Boston: Little, Brown, 1956), p. 70.
4. Kenneth Allott and Miriam Farris, *The Art of Graham Greene* (New York: Russell, 1963), p. 15.
5. Evelyn Waugh, "Felix Culpa?" *Commonweal*, July 16, 1948, p. 323.
6. David Pryce-Jones, *Graham Greene* (Edinburgh: Oliver and Boyd, 1963), p. 29.
7. John Atkins, *Graham Greene* (London: Calder and Boyars, 1966), p. 124.

184

3. ETERTAINMENTS

1. Cited in Pryce-Jones, *Graham Greene*, p. 62.
2. Allott and Farris, *The Art of Graham Greene*, pp. 78–79.
3. Pryce-Jones, *Graham Greene*, p. 18.
4. Atkins, *Graham Greene*, p. 31.
5. Ibid., p. 242.

4. SHORT STORIES

1. Gwenn R. Boardman, *Graham Greene: The Aesthetics of Exploration* (Gainesville: University of Florida Press, 1971), p. 160.

5. PLAYS

1. Atkins, *Graham Greene*, p. 254.

Bibliography

WORKS BY GRAHAM GREENE

Babbling April. Oxford: Blackwell, 1925.
The Man Within. London: Heinemann, 1929.
The Name of Action. London: Heinemann, 1930.
Rumour at Nightfall. London: Heinemann, 1931.
Stamboul Train. London: Heinemann, 1932.
It's a Battlefield. London: Heinemann, 1934.
The Basement Room. London: Cresset, 1935.
England Made Me. London: Heinemann, 1935.
A Gun for Sale. London: Heinemann, 1936.
Journey without Maps. London: Heinemann, 1936.
Brighton Rock. London: Heinemann, 1938.
The Confidential Agent, London: Heinemann, 1939.
The Lawless Roads. London: Longmans, Green, 1939.
The Power and the Glory. London: Heinemann, 1940.
The Ministry of Fear. London: Heinemann, 1943.
Nineteen Stories. London: Heinemann, 1947.
The Heart of the Matter. London: Heinemann, 1948.
The Third Man. London: Heinemann, 1950.
The End of the Affair. London: Heinemann, 1951.
The Lost Childhood and Other Essays. London: Eyre and
    Spottiswoode, 1951.
The Living Room. London: Heinemann, 1953.
Twenty-One Stories. London: Heinemann, 1954.
Loser Takes All. London: Heinemann, 1955.
The Quiet American. London: Heinemann, 1955.
Our Man in Havana. London: Heinemann, 1958.
The Potting Shed. London: Heinemann, 1958.

The Complaisant Lover. London: Heinemann, 1959.
A Burnt-Out Case. London: Heinemann, 1961.
In Search of a Character: Two African Journals. London: Bodley Head, 1961.
A Sense of Reality. London: Bodley Head, 1963.
Carving a Statue. London: Bodley Head, 1964.
The Comedians. London: Bodley Head, 1966.
May We Borrow Your Husband? London: Bodley Head, 1967.
Collected Essays. London: Bodley Head, 1969.
Travels with My Aunt. London: Bodley Head, 1969.
A Sort of Life. London: Bodley Head, 1971.
Collected Stories. London: Bodley Head, 1972.
The Pleasure-Dome: The Collected Film Criticism 1935–40. John Russell Taylor, ed. London: Secker and Warburg, 1972.
The Honorary Consul. London: Bodley Head, 1973.
Lord Rochester's Monkey. London: Bodley Head, 1974.
The Return of A. J. Raffles. London: Bodley Head, 1975.
The Human Factor. London: Bodley Head, 1978.
Doctor Fischer of Geneva or the Bomb Party. London: Bodley Head, 1980.
Ways of Escape. London: Bodley Head, 1980.
J'Accuse. London: Bodley Head, 1982.
Monsignor Quixote. London: Bodley Head, 1982.

WORKS ABOUT GRAHAM GREENE
(*denotes works of especial interest or significance)

Allain, Marie-Françoise. *The Other Man: Conversations with Graham Greene*. New York: Simon and Schuster, 1983.
*Allen, Walter. "The Novels of Graham Greene." *Penguin New Writing, 18*. Harmondsworth, England: Penguin, 1943, pp. 148–60.
*Allott, Kenneth, and Miriam Farris. *The Art of Graham Greene*. New York: Russell, 1963.
*Atkins, John. *Graham Greene*. London: Calder and Boyars, 1966.

Boardman, Gwenn R. *Graham Greene: The Aesthetics of Exploration*. Gainesville: University of Florida Press, 1971.

DeVitis, A. A. *Graham Greene*. New York: Twayne, 1964.

Evans, Robet Owen, ed. *Graham Greene: Some Critical Considerations*. Lexington: University of Kentucky Press, 1963.

Hynes, Samuel L., ed. *Graham Greene: A Collection of Critical Essays*. Englewood Cliffs, N.J.: Prentice-Hall, 1973.

Kohn, Lynette. *Graham Greene: The Major Novels*. Palo Alto, Calif.: Stanford Honors Essays in Humanities IV, 1961.

Kunkel, F. L. *The Labyrinthine Ways of Graham Greene*. New York: Sheed and Ward, 1959.

*Lerner, Laurence. "Graham Greene." *Critical Quarterly* V (Autumn 1963), 217–31.

Lewis, R. W. B. "Graham Greene: The Religious Affair." *The Picaresque Saint*. Philadelphia: Lippincott, 1959, pp. 220–74.

———. "The 'Trilogy.'" *Graham Greene, The Power and the Glory, Text, Background, and Criticism*. R. W. B. Lewis and Peter J. Conn, eds. New York: Viking, 1970, pp. 373–94.

Lodge, David. *Graham Greene*. New York: Columbia University Press, 1966.

Mesnet, Marie-Beatrice. *Graham Greene and the Heart of the Matter*. London: Cresset, 1954.

Miller, Robert H. *Graham Greene, A Descriptive Catalog*. Lexington: University of Kentucky Press, 1979.

*O'Faoláin, Seán. "Graham Greene: I Suffer, Therefore I Am." *The Vanishing Hero: Studies in the Novelists of the Twenties*. Boston: Little, Brown, 1956, pp. 45–72.

*Phillips, Gene D. *Graham Greene: The Films of His Fiction*. New York: Teachers College Press, 1974.

Pryce-Jones, David. *Graham Greene*. Edinburgh: Oliver and Boyd, 1963.

Spurling, John. *Graham Greene*. London: Methuen, 1983.

Stratford, Philip. *Faith and Fiction: Creative Process in Greene and Mauriac.* Notre Dame, Ind.: University of Notre Dame Press, 1964.

Turnell, Martin. *Graham Greene: A Critical Essay.* Grand Rapids, Mich.: Erdmans, 1967.

*Wobbe, R. A. *Graham Greene, A Bibliography and Guide to Research.* New York: Garland, 1979.

Wolfe, Peter. *Graham Greene the Entertainer.* Carbondale: Southern Illinois University Press, 1972.

Wyndham, Francis. *Graham Greene.* London: Longmans, Green, 1955.

*Zabel, Morton Dauwen. *Craft and Character in Modern Fiction.* New York: Viking Press, 1957, pp. 276–96.

Index